A PRIMER FOR PICKLES
a reader for relishes

By Ruby Charity Stark Guthrie
& Jack Stark Guthrie

Drawings by Richard Calvo

101 Productions
San Francisco
1974

TO PEREGRINE PICKLE

Copyright © 1974 by Ruby Charity Stark Guthrie and Jack Stark Guthrie
Drawings © 1974 by Richard Calvo

Printed in the United States of America

Distributed to the Book Trade in the United States
by Charles Scribner's Sons, New York and in Canada
by Van Nostrand Reinhold, Ltd., Toronto

Published by 101 Productions
834 Mission Street
San Francisco, California 94103

Library of Congress Cataloging in Publication Data

Guthrie, Ruby Charity Stark, 1898—
    A primer for pickles & a reader for relishes.

    1.   Pickles.   2.   Cookery (Relishes)   I.   Guthrie,
Jack Stark, joint author.   II.   Title.
TX805.G87   641.4'6   74-18029
ISBN 0-912238-53-4
ISBN 0-912238-52-6   (pbk.)

Contents

75—16679

Prologue

"Where there are no pickles, the people perish."

Researching family recipes can be filled with surprises. Geneological ghosts, geniuses and rotters appear without proper invitations, but all should be welcomed. There are really no recipes for families, thank heavens, and if in the future through genetic jugging this occurs, life will become a dull feast.

Although it still remains to be fully researched and documented, it is our fancy that in a remote Vermont or New Hampshire hamlet, the Starks merged (if that is the word) with the Pickles. There is some indication not only of that, but an ancient French or Spanish connection with the Piccalillis (not to be confused with the Peccadillos of Picadors), but the origin of the name is related to the Smalls, Pierces and Slashes. (We have yet to establish the relationship between these families with the Chutneys and the Relishes, but perhaps in the sequel to this book—now tentatively entitled *Sons and Daughters of the American Pickles* and *Daughters of the American Relish*—we hope to do so.)

That this will be important for historical thought there is no doubt, for the Pickles are almost totally ignored in *Bartlett's Familiar Quotations* except when they are dealt with in a pejorative way: i.e., *pickled,* to get into a *pickle,* etc. Oh yes, Bartlett kindly deals with the Pied Piper, Jack Horner (under *Pie*) and their ilk, but not one Pickle is mentioned between *Pickwickian* and *Pigmy.* A grievous oversight, indeed. That Bartlett could ignore the modern (1620-?) ancestor of the Pickles, Peregrine Pickle, is understandable. True to his name, Peregrine, he was a wanderer who as a Puritan Pickle settled near Salem. But for Bartlett to ignore his grandson, who was immortalized in Tobias Smollett's great English novel, *The Adventures of Peregrine Pickle* (1751), passes understanding. Thus, many of the quotations sprinkled throughout this book are designed to force the new editors of *Bartlett's* to correct this oversight, however belatedly.

To that end, under the portrait of the original Peregrine Pickle (found in an old family album with some other family likenesses) we have printed his best line, most deserving of quotation. We have further taken a few harmless liberties with some other familiar quotations so that at least one of them might be accepted for a new edition of Bartlett's otherwise most edifying collection. Until that great time (and, of course, after), Pickles, wherever you are, be proud.

Ruby Charity Stark Guthrie
Jack Stark Guthrie

Spokane & San Francisco
1974

There is no great problem to pickling, unless it be poetry, which is indeed a mystery. The art, the alchemy, the psychology, the poetry of pickling, as of any cooking, need love. As Alexander Pope, that great 18th century English poet and psychologist (long before the word was commonly used), puts it:

> . . . Look round our world; behold the chain of love
> Combining all below and all above,
> See plastic nature working to this end,
> The single atoms each to other tend,
> Attract, attracted to, the next in place
> Formed and impelled its neighbor to embrace.
> See matter next, with various life endued,
> Press to one centre still, the general good.
> See dying vegetables life sustain,
> See life dissolving vegetate again:
> All forms perish other forms supply
> (By turns we catch the vital breath, and die)
> Like bubbles on the sea of matter born,
> They rise, they break, and to that sea return.
> Nothing is foreign: parts relate to whole;
> One all-extending, all-preserving soul
> Connects each being, greatest with the least;
> Made beast in aid of man, and man of beast;
> All served, all-serving: nothing stands alone;
> The chain holds on, and where it ends, unknown.

And as is so in all things: If you don't have love, and can't combine, do not try the pickle vine. But if you do, be a Juliet to your pickles, and a Lady Macbeth (with some reservations) to your grocer or wholesale producer. Demand cucumbers, vegetables and fruits as fresh as possible from harvesting, preferably 24 hours after picking. Failing this, if you are not a gardener, search out a friendly farmer.

INGREDIENTS

In any event choose good quality ingredients, uniform in size and age and free of blemishes. Misfits can be used for relishes. Cucumbers should be left with a stem 1/4 to 1/2 inch long. If you pick them yourself, just pinch off the vine with your fingernail. Fruits may be not quite ripe; in fact, they make better pickles.

The ordinary cucumbers found in most markets are called "slicers" and are for table use, not for pickling. The best pickles are made from the black spine types, with small black prickles, such as the Chicago Pickling Cucumber. (Other varieties are listed under the XYZ's of Gardening.)

Wash all ingredients carefully to remove bacteria which might spoil your product. In washing cucumbers, don't *scrub* so that you remove the black prickles. A good way to get off the dirt and bacteria is to soak them for a *few* minutes in a dishpan with a tablespoon of pickling salt and one of vinegar. Rinse well in running water as you gently rub them.

UTENSILS

Witches may have gotten away with using an iron pot, but remember what they were cooking. Never use brass, copper, iron or galvanized utensils. Any of these will produce strange tastes and undesirable color changes because the metals will react with the vinegar and salt solutions. Use enameled ware, glass, aluminum, stainless steel or stoneware utensils only. Stir with a wooden spoon and dip out the ingredients with a non-metal cup or a slotted stainless steel spoon.

WATER

Whenever possible, use soft water free of minerals. Some water-softening devices *add* minerals. Check the name of your device and call the nearest branch office of the U.S. Bureau of Agriculture, your local paper's home economist, or a college or university department of home economics for advice.

Also check to see how heavily your water is chlorinated. Call your city's water department. If you can't get the information you need, plan in advance and boil the water you'll need for 15 minutes. Let it stand for 24 hours. When all the sediment has settled to the bottom, skim the top and ladle the water from the top. Strain through several layers of cloth if need be. Add 1 tablespoon of vinegar to each gallon of water before using. Always follow this procedure with hard water too.

If all else fails, use bottled distilled water with vinegar added in the same quantity as to boiled water.

You will never regret all this effort.

SALT

Do not use table salt in pickling cucumbers. You can use it in pickle relishes if you like, but why? All table salts have been sold to us for their flowing qualities. True, they flow because they are laced with starch or carbonates or bicarbonates of sodium, magnesium or calcium. These additives, including iodine in iodized salt, will darken the brine and soften the pickles. So, if you have a good dairy, pickling, kosher or pure granulated salt on hand, use it not only in your pickles, but in your relishes as well.

Pound for pound, granulated and flake salts have the same strength, but they are not equal in weight-to-volume ratio. When using a flake salt (kosher or dairy), you should double the amount of granulated pickling salt called for in the recipe. Your best buy, therefore, is a good pickling salt.

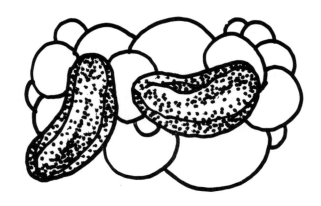

SUGAR

White granulated sugar is used in all recipes unless brown sugar is specified or if you desire a darker color. The sweetening powers of each differ because of bulk. Check the weight-to-bulk table for equivalents, or use weight measurements.

VINEGAR

Vinegar should be of 40 to 60 percent grain strength; that is, from 4 to 6 percent acidity. Check for this on the label. Vinegars of unknown strength should not be used. Either cider or white distilled vinegar free of sediment may be used. When pickling light-colored foods such as onions, white distilled vinegar is preferable for it will not darken the ingredients.

When making a simple solution of vinegar, salt and water, do not boil more than 5 to 6 minutes unless otherwise directed in the recipe. Long boiling weakens vinegar. Follow the timings suggested in the recipes; if a recipe says bring just to boil, do that.

SPICES, HERBS & BULBS

Always use fresh spices and herbs. Old ones will discolor the product and produce musty, strange flavors. If called for in the recipe, tie spices in a muslin bag which is large enough to allow the pickling liquid to flow through during the cooking period. Remove the bag before canning (although some old recipes call for its retention). Any recipe can be changed to fit individual tastes in spices. Blended pickling spices are available commercially, but if you wish to mix your own, the following is a list of commonly used pickling spices:

Allspice	Cardamom	Cinnamon stick	Dill seed	Mustard seed
Bay leaf	Cayenne	Coriander seed	Ginger	Nutmeg (grated)
Black pepper	Chili	Clove	Mace	Hot red pepper

GARLIC Over the centuries, this marvelous bulb, which in Latin means *spear-leek*, has been attributed magical powers and medicinal potency. Whether or not the stories are true, it is the most pungent of the onion family, and used with care can be a great addition to any pickle recipe. But one warning: If you wish to put cloves of garlic into jars, such as in garlic dills, peel the cloves then plunge them into boiling water first for about 1 minute. This blanching process kills the bacteria so common to the onion family which can cause spoilage. Or, if you wish, place the cloves in the vinegar solution you will pour over the pickles about 1 minute before filling the jars.

DILL An umbelliferous plant whose family name is semantically very distinguished. It is related to umbrella and shade because its flowers stem in a circle from a single center. The cluster at the top of the stalk is called the dill head; it is best when its seeds are fully grown but not falling off the stalk. Dill has long been the center for many pickle recipes, and deservedly so. It is easily grown, so check under the XYZ's of Gardening for Pickles for instructions. Good dill is difficult to buy.

HORSERADISH ROOT Strictly viewed, horseradish is the root of an herb of the mustard family, but rather than sticking with the narrow botanical view, let us just call it in the common parlance a root rather than an herb. After being blanched (as in the treatment of garlic), the root, whether grated or left whole, adds a piquancy to any pickle recipe. Also, when placed whole in the jar, it keeps pickles firm. If you buy commercially prepared horseradish, be sure to get the unadulterated variety which is made only with vinegar and salt.

HORSERADISH LEAVES Like the roots, the leaves will aid in keeping pickles firm; wash carefully and add to jar. Grape or cherry leaves may also be used.

CABBAGE LEAVES If you put cabbage leaves between green pickles while heating, it will green them. Another way is to heat them in strong ginger tea. Of course, ordinary food colorings can also be used.

ALUM AND LIME

ALUM Alum has fallen into some disrepute in modern recipes, for a touch too much can make the product bitter. However, when properly used it is excellent for crisping. When it is called for in this book, the amount has been tested for years; therefore follow instructions exactly. A good way to test for the proper amount of alum is as follows: Dissolve specified quantity of alum in warm water before soaking pickles. Taste the alum-water solution; if it is so bitter that your mouth puckers *too much,* dilute with water until you only pucker a *little.* In very old recipes, it will often say to use a piece of alum the size of a nut (about a scant level teaspoon). In general, use alum according to the following proportions: 1/4 to 1/2 teaspoon of alum to 1 quart of vinegar and 3 quarts of water. Remember, it takes a small amount of alum to harden pickles; therefore, be conservative! When in doubt use less.

LIME When lime is called for, the recipe is referring to calcium oxide, obtainable in most drug stores (as is alum). Lime is also used for crisping pickles and can be substituted for alum. Use 1 tablespoon of calcium oxide to 1 quart of soft water.

After stirring well, allow the solution to settle. Use the clear portion to cover pickles. Soak for 2 hours, drain and proceed with the recipe as directed.

BRINES AND BRINING

A brine is a solution of salt and water, preferably soft water. Brines draw natural sugars and moistures from food to form lactic acid which protects them from spoilage bacteria.

A simple test for a strong brine (about 10 percent), if called for in a recipe, is this: Place a 2-ounce egg in the bottom of a crock. Mix 1 cup of pickling salt to 5 cups of water. If the egg rises, the solution is strong enough.

A weak brine is 1 cup of pickling salt to 9 cups of water. This brine will cause quicker fermentation, but unless the scum that rises is constantly skimmed off and the brine clear, pickles kept in this brine will spoil in a few weeks. Pickles will spoil

if not kept completely under any brine. About 1/2 gallon of brine will cover a gallon of cucumbers (6 pounds or 50 medium, whole).

Brining is particularly important to cure pickles for future use. For the gardener it is a great boon because pickles can be picked each day and "put down." When wanted they can be turned into dill, sweet, sour or almost any pickle he or she wishes.

Leave 1/4- to 1/2-inch stems on cucumbers. Carefully wash without removing prickles (see washing instructions); then put them into a large stone crock. Make a brine of 2 quarts of water to 2 cups of pickling salt. Boil, skim until clear, then cool. Fill the crock with enough brine to cover the pickles. When ready to use, soak in cold water until freshened.

Most pickles are done by the short-brining method, which uses a strong brine for only 24 hours, rather than by the long-brining one described above. The appropriate method is indicated in each recipe.

PROCESSING AND CANNING

Most of the recipes in this book do not call for subjecting the sealed jars to a boiling water bath or using a pressure canner. The exceptions are some of the recipes with much sugar, such as pickled fruits, and some vegetable ones.

The reason for this omission is simple: The old-timers simply didn't believe in a boiling water bath for pickling. They didn't believe in it because subjecting pickles to a hot water bath raises the temperature in the jars to 180°. This could cook them too much, resulting in flabby pickles, and who wants a flabby pickle!

Upon the subject of the bath, there is some disagreement among pickle experts. Many modern ones believe it is necessary in order to kill all spoilage bacteria. Our experience is that not only is the bath not needed in most pickle recipes (because of the high acidity and salt content of pickled products), but if canning directions are religiously followed, spoilage will seldom occur without the bath. According to experts in the San Francisco office of the U.S. Department of Agriculture, the danger of contracting botulism, for example, is miniscule in properly pickled and canned products.

Spoilage will occur without the bath if the proper solution of salt and vinegar hasn't been used; if canning instructions concerning the sterilization of jars and lids and cooking utensils haven't been followed; if the product hasn't been carefully washed; or if the lids haven't been properly sealed.

For those who wish to use the boiling water bath, the timing is given in some recipes and is anywhere from 5 to 25 minutes, counting from the time the water boils. *If no timing is given in the recipe, follow this general rule: When you use the hot water bath, allow 5 to 15 minutes when the product is packed in pints or quarts and 25 minutes when packed in half-gallons.* In high altitudes, for each 1000 feet above sea level add 1 minute more of boiling time if the total time is 20 minutes or less. Add 2 minutes per 1000 feet if the time is more than 20 minutes. For using a pressure cooker canner, follow the manufacturer's instruction booklet explicitly.

TIMING GUIDE FOR HOT WATER BATH PROCESS

PICKLES AND RELISHES
Bread and Butter
   quarts: 10 minutes
   pints: 5 minutes
Chutney
   pints: 5 minutes
Cross Cut Slices
   pints: 5 minutes
Dill Green Beans
   pints: 5 minutes

Gherkins, Sweet
   pints: 5 minutes
Piccalilli
   pints: 5 minutes
Pepper-Onion Relish
   pints: 5 minutes
Relish, Corn
   pints: 15 minutes
Watermelon
   pints: 5 minutes

Start counting processing time as soon as water returns to boil.

FRUIT PICKLES
Peaches
   quarts or pints: 20 minutes
Pears
   quarts or pints: 20 minutes

PICKLES, DILL
Fermented (whole)
   quarts: 15 minutes
Unfermented (whole)
   quarts: 20 minutes

A regular hot water canner, a clean laundry boiler with a tight-fitting lid, any utensil with a lid which is high enough so that the jars will be completely covered by the bath can be used. Place a wooden rack on the bottom of the utensil so that the jars will not crack from too much heat. Never allow them to touch one another or the sides of the container. Allow about a 2-inch space between jars. Fill the container up with water to just about jar height. Lower the jars into the warming water. (Never put jars into boiling or near-boiling water; it may crack them.) Cover completely with more water. Remember to count from the time the water covering the jars begins to boil. Continue to add water if it boils away. Always make sure the lid on the container is tight. Remove the jars with tongs; never touch the lids. Place the processed jars out of a draft which might crack them, upright on a pad of paper or rack and allow to cool for about 12 hours. Do not disturb. If they are properly sealed, the lids will give off with a "ting" when tapped with a spoon or knife. Tighten rings if necessary and store in a cool place. If not properly sealed or if the produce is touching the lid, you will hear a dull note. Reprocess product at once using a new lid.

Actually, according to an expert home economist with the U.S. Department of Agriculture, the hot water bath process is recommended in so many pickle recipes largely for the novice who may not have carefully followed the recipe or the rules of

canning. For example, not sterilizing utensils such as spoons can spoil an otherwise perfect batch.

By all means use the hot water bath process or pressure canner if you feel insecure about your canning procedures. You will feel secure, however, if you focus upon the demands of the recipe, plus cleanliness and proper sterilization.

And now to simple canning.

Check jars for nicks or other defects. If you do use the hot water bath process or a pressure canner, this inspection is particularly important to prevent accidents. Find out if your jars will take heats from 180° to a pressure canner's 240°. Next, place your jars in water to cover and boil 20 minutes at least to sterilize them. Always leave your jars in the hot water until ready to use. When you are ready to spoon or dip out the pickled product, sterilize the utensils you are using.

Unless otherwise instructed in the recipe, fill the jars with the pickled produce to about 1/2 inch from the top. This is called headspace. Then make certain the liquid solution called for is poured to the top of the jar. Pass a knife over the top to remove bubbles. Seal immediately. Do one jar at a time in the filling and sealing procedure.

Some books call for glass lids and separate rubbers. We find the vacuum type with the screw rings the easiest to use. Simply follow the manufacturer's directions for boiling, placement and tightening. Before sealing, make certain to wipe off the lip of the jar with a *clean* cloth. Follow the instructions given in the hot-bath process for allowing the jars to cool, the tightening of lids, and storage. Label and date.

Unless the recipe specifies otherwise, sealed jars should be allowed to stand in a cool, dark place for several months before using. The longer you wait, the more thoroughly blended and permeated will the flavors be. Once the jars are stored, keep an eye on them. If spoilage appears, do not eat the contents or even taste them. Dispose of them in such a way that neither animal nor human can touch them.

Signs of spoilage are: a bulging lid, leakage, disagreeable odor, mold, change in color, spurting liquid, or an unusual slipperiness or mushiness of the pickled product. Empty the jar and wash in a hot soapy water. Rinse and sterilize in boiling water for 15 minutes.

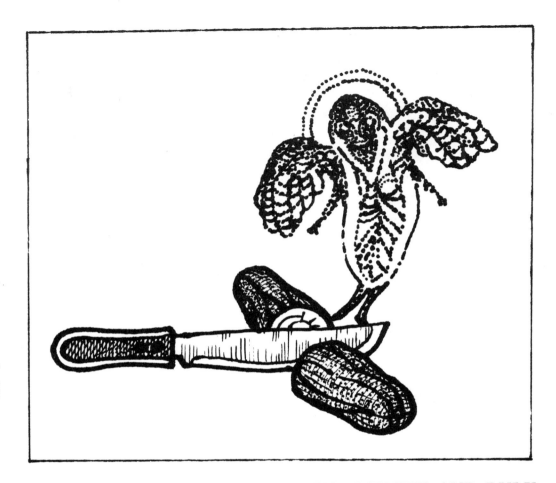

THE RELATIONSHIP BETWEEN THE WEIGHT AND BULK
OF INGREDIENTS TO BE PICKLED

Because all vegetables and fruits vary in size, season, age, water content and the climates they were raised in, it is impossible to produce exact measurements relating weight to bulk. The quantities called for in each recipe, therefore, should only be considered approximate, but they are close enough to allow the housewife to purchase about what is needed. In general, however, it is always wise to purchase more rather than less. Whatever is left over can always be turned into a relish or jam, or the imaginative cook might invent a new recipe.

It is also because of the measurement problem that you will find some of the recipes in this book do not list the quantity the ingredients will produce after processing. Well, you can always boil more jars. And if you get confused between quarts, pounds, etc., use a jar to measure what you need! The major rule for pickling, in any event, is to use the right vinegar and salt or sugar solutions. You can always vary the ingredients and spices.

The old English terms of wine glasses, coffeecupfuls, gills, pecks and bushels are defined here in modern terms for those historically oriented, enterprising cooks who may be puzzled by them in old cookbooks.

Do not confuse dry measure pints and quarts with liquid measure pints and quarts. Dry measure is about 1/6 larger than liquid, and is used when dealing with large quantities of fruits and vegetables.

A TABLE OF WEIGHTS AND MEASURES

LIQUID MEASURES
A pinch, dash or few grains = about 1/8 teaspoon
60 drops = 1 teaspoon
1 teaspoon = 1/3 tablespoon
1 tablespoon = 3 teaspoons
2 tablespoons = 1 fluid ounce
4 tablespoons = 1/4 cup
8 tablespoons = 1/2 cup
16 tablespoons = 1 cup or 8 fluid ounces
2 cups = 1 pint
1 gill, liquid = 1/2 cup or 4 fluid ounces
1 pint, liquid = 4 gills or 16 fluid ounces
1 quart, liquid = 2 pints
1 gallon, liquid = 4 quarts

SUGARS, SACCHARIN AND SALT
Sugar, white granulated:
    1 pound = 2 cups
Sugar, brown: 1 pound = 2-1/4 to 2-3/4 cups, packed
Sugar, powdered: 1 pound = 3-1/2 to 4 cups; 4 to 4-1/2 cups, sifted
Saccharin: 1-1/4 grain tablet = 1 teaspoon sugar
Salt: 1 tablespoon = 1 ounce

DRY MEASURES
1 dry quart = 2 dry pints or 1/8 peck
1 peck = 8 dry quarts or 16 dry pints
1 bushel = 4 pecks or 32 dry quarts

OLD TERMS
4 tablespoonsful = 1 wine glass, 1/2 gill or 1/4 cup
2 wine glasses = 1 gill (same for dry measure), 1/2 cup, 8 tablespoonsful or 4 ounces
2 gills = 1 coffeecupful, 16 tablespoons or 8 ounces

Follow the recipes carefully or you'll get witch's pickles: shriveled, hollow or slippery. They'll shrivel if there was too strong a vinegar, sugar or salt solution, if they were overcooked or overprocessed. They'll be hollow if the cucumbers were too old. They'll be slippery if there was too little salt or acid, if the seal was not airtight, or if the garlic and spices were moldy.
Remember, carefulness is all!

**CHARGE ON! CHARGE ON! PICKLES EXCELSIOR!
AND SING TO ANY TUNE YOU LIKE THIS SONG:**

Green grow the pickles, O;
   Green grow the pickles, O;
The sweetest hours that e'er I spend,
   Are spent among the pickles, O!

Auld Nature swears, the lovely dears
   Her noblest work she classes, O;
Her prentice han' she tried on man,
   An' then she made the pickles, O.

(Apologies to Robert Burns)

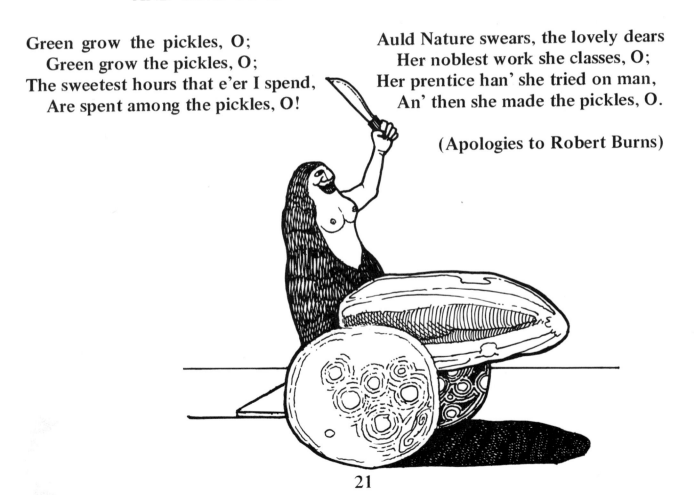

21

Catsups & chutneys

WORLDLY CATSUP

"Life is short; this catsup briefer."—Anon.

2 quarts finely chopped tomatoes with
    liquid or, preferably, home-canned
    tomatoes

1 onion, cut finely
1 to 2 tablespoons pickling salt
3 tablespoons brown sugar, packed

Boil until quite thick, stirring frequently. Strain through a sieve, working it all through but the seeds. Return to stove and add:

2 tablespoons dry mustard
1 tablespoon whole allspice
1 tablespoon ground black pepper
1 tablespoon ground cinnamon

1 teaspoon ground cloves
1/2 teaspoon cayenne
1 small nutmeg, grated
1 pint cider vinegar

Boil, stirring often so that catsup does not burn, until it will just run from the mouth of a bottle. Pour hot into a sterilized large-mouthed bottle. Seal according to directions in ABC's.

Makes about 1 quart

23

CELESTIAL CATSUP

According to the *Oxford Universal Dictionary*, the word catchup or catsup came into our language in 1690 and ketchup in 1711 from the Chinese *koechiap* or *ke-tsiap* which means the brine of a pickled fish. No doubt something was lost in the translation to tomato.

In honor of the word's origins, we have chosen the name Celestial Catsup to recall the Celestial Kingdom of China and also to indicate that our recipe is not only celestial in taste, but also as basic as the sun with other satellite recipes for catsups circling about it. Vary this recipe and you'll discover them. Try the non-tomato-based catsups for other cosmic adventures.

12 to 13 pounds tomatoes (about 8 quarts), washed and cut into small pieces
10 medium-sized onions, sliced
2 long red peppers, seeds and membranes removed
10 medium-sized apples, peeled, cored and sliced

Simmer these ingredients until soft. Strain them through a colander and sieve. Add:

3/4 cup brown sugar, packed
1 tablespoon paprika
following spices tied in muslin bag:
1 tablespoon each whole allspice, celery
   seed, cloves, mace and peppercorns

2 inches stick cinnamon
1 nutmeg, finely grated
1/2 teaspoon dry mustard
1 clove garlic, chopped
2 small bay leaves

These spices may be infinitely varied. Boil rapidly without scorching, stirring often, about 1-1/2 hours or until thick and reduced to half. Remove spice bag and add:

1 pint cider vinegar
1 to 2 tablespoons pickling salt

cayenne and horseradish (optional)

Simmer and adjust to taste. Boil 10 minutes longer or until thick. Put in sterilized jars while hot and seal according to directions in ABC's. Or, put in bottles, cork and seal with sealing wax.
Makes about 5 quarts

GARDEN OF EDEN GREEN TOMATO CATSUP

"The recipe for perpetual ignorance is:
be satisfied with your garden and content with your catsup."
—Elbert Hubble

12 to 13 pounds green tomatoes, sliced

2 large onions, sliced
pickling salt to taste

Place vegetables in layers, sprinkling pickling salt between; let stand 24 hours. Drain and rinse. Place in pot and add:

1/2 cup mustard seed
2 tablespoons whole allspice
2 tablespoons whole cloves
2 tablespoons dry mustard
2 tablespoons ground ginger

2 tablespoons black pepper
2 teaspoons celery seed
1/4 pound brown sugar (about
    5/8 cup, packed)
enough vinegar to cover the ingredients
    well

Boil 2 hours or until reduced to half, carefully stirring from time to time. Strain through a sieve and pour in sterilized wide-mouth jars. Seal according to directions in ABC's.
Makes about 5 quarts

APRÈS L'ÉDEN APPLE CATSUP

How . . . escape from his ancestors or draw off from his veins the black drop which he drew from his father's or his mother's life? It often appears in a family, as if all the qualities of the progenitors were potted in several jars—some ruling quality in each son or daughter of the house—and sometimes the unmixed temperment, the rank unmitigated elixir, the family vice, is drawn off in a separate individual, and the others are proportionally relieved.

—Ralph Waldo Emerson, *Conduct of Life*

This potted child of Eden is of the non-rank, mitigated (from the Latin *mitis* mild + *agere* to do) variety of elixirs.

". . . ask not for a larger garden /But for finer seeds."—Russell Herman Cornwell

1 dozen tart apples, peeled, cored and quartered
1 cup sugar
1 teaspoon black pepper
1 teaspoon ground cloves

1 teaspoon dry mustard
2 teaspoons ground cinnamon
2 medium-size onions, chopped *very* fine
1 tablespoon pickling salt, or to taste
1 pint cider vinegar

Stew apples until soft in as little water as possible. Pass through a sieve. (You should have about a quart of sieved apple.) Add the sugar, spices and onion; stir all together and add the salt and the vinegar, adjusting to taste. Boil carefully 1 hour, stirring frequently. When about as thick as tomato catsup and very hot, pour in sterilized wide-mouthed bottles. Seal according to directions in ABC's. Quantity depends upon the type of apples.

CURRANT CATSUP

4 pounds currants
2 pounds sugar
1 pint white or cider vinegar

1 teaspoon whole cloves
1 tablespoon ground cinnamon
pepper and allspice to taste

Combine all ingredients and boil until thoroughly cooked. Strain all but the skins through a sieve. Boil down until just thick enough to run freely from the mouth of a bottle. Pour hot into bottles and cork. Keep refrigerated.

TOMATO AND PEAR CHUTNEY

1 pound tomatoes, chopped
1 pound pears, peeled and chopped
1 green bell pepper, seeded and chopped
1 cup seeded raisins, chopped
1 onion, chopped
1/2 teaspoon dry mustard

1/8 teaspoon cayenne
1/2 teaspoon ground ginger
1 teaspoon table salt
1 cup brown sugar, packed
1 4-ounce can pimiento, chopped

Combine all ingredients except the pimiento. Boil slowly for about 1 hour, stirring occasionally. Add pimiento and boil 5 minutes longer. Pour into sterilized jars while hot and seal according to directions in ABC's.

ELIZA DOOLITTLE'S APPLE CHUTNEY

12 large sour apples
1 sweet red pepper, minced
1 pint cider vinegar
3 cups brown sugar, packed
juice of 4 lemons

2 green bell peppers, seeded and minced
1 cup seeded raisins, chopped
1 tablespoon ground ginger
1/4 cup chopped mint leaves
1/2 teaspoon cayenne
1 tablespoon table salt

Pare, core and chop apples. Put all the ingredients together in the order given. Simmer until thick. Pour into sterilized jars while hot and seal according to directions in ABC's.

Dill pickles

LOT'S WIFE'S ROCK SALT DILLS

This is the type of recipe you'll always look back and forward to! It is so flexible, unlike its namesake, that no set quantity of cucumbers need be used. For the home gardener it is a real boon because cucumbers can be picked as they become dill-size, about 3 to 4 inches. And the very busy cook who buys a small quantity of cucumbers at a time can put them up quickly. Use:

dill-size, 4-inch cucumbers

Wash cucumbers. Pierce each on both ends and in the middle with a clean ice pick or knitting needle. This allows the liquid to seep through and prevents hollow or mushy pickles. Put in the bottom of each quart jar:

1 rounded tablespoon rock salt (While this is generally available at large markets and health-food stores, check on the ingredients listed on the package, because some of it is labeled "inedible" and is only for making ice cream.)

1 large grape leaf or horseradish leaf
2 to 3 dill heads
2 hot red peppers
1 clove garlic, peeled and blanched

Pack cucumbers in sterilized jars. Reserve space for more dill heads on top. Fill jars with *cold* purified water. Seal according to directions in ABC's. If you don't heat lids, tighten firmly.

Gently turn jar up and down until the rock salt has dissolved. Store in a cool place. They will be ready in about 2 or 3 months. You may note some fermentation for a few days which is natural for this method of pickling. If a jar runs over, wait until the fermentation is over and reseal.

DISRAELI'S PARLIAMENT OF PICKLED (KOSHER?) DILLS

We have never understood how a pickle could become kosher; however, it is fitting that this recipe bears the name Disraeli (originally d'Israeli), Britain's first prime minister of Jewish extraction, and Queen Victoria's favorite one. It is said that she could not conceive of Gladstone, her most unfavorite one, having his name connected to any pickle, not even a Protestant one. She couldn't stomach the man or the idea, but thought his name aptly fitted the Gladstone bag. Enough history for the nonce. Queen Victoria, whom Disraeli called his Faery Queen, is further glorified by this recipe.

Yes, this is an apt title in other ways as well. This is the *long* pickling process for dillys, a condition that parliaments and congresses of men share with them, as they, too, struggle in stone crocks towards culture and maturity with condiments, constituents, syrups, etc.

40 cucumbers (4-inch)
3 tablespoons pickling spices
dill, to individual taste
2 gallons hot purified water
1-1/2 cups pickling salt
1 pint white or cider vinegar

peppercorns to individual taste, but at
    least 1 per jar
horseradish roots or leaves, enough for
    each jar (about 1-inch piece root or
    1 large leaf)
garlic to individual taste, but at least
    1 clove per jar

Continued on following page

Carefully wash and dry cucumbers so as not to remove the spines. In a large stone crock, put 1/2 the mixed spices *only*. Put down a layer of dill. Add cucumbers. Put the remaining spices and dill on top of the cucumbers.

To the hot water add the salt and vinegar. Stir until the salt is dissolved. Cool the brine and pour it over the cucumbers. Cover with a glass pie plate or a dinner one. Put on the plate a weight, such as a stone, heavy enough to hold the plate beneath the brine. It is very important that this be done. Otherwise, with such a weak brining solution the pickles will spoil. During curing add more brine if necessary.

It is equally important to keep the temperature of the crock between 68° and 72° for 2 to 4 weeks. Remove the fermentation scum each day. When the pickles are an even olive color without any white spots and well flavored, they are ready for packing in boiled jars.

Now place at least 1 peppercorn and horseradish leaf (if using) in each jar. Pierce each pickle on the ends and once in the middle with a sterilized ice pick or knitting needle. Make a new brine of:

1 gallon hot purified water   1 cup white or cider vinegar
3/4 cup pickling salt

Put in horseradish roots (if using) and peeled garlic. Bring to boil. This process will remove the bacteria from the horseradish roots and garlic which might spoil your pickles.

Place cucumbers in sterilized jars. Pour the hot brine over pickles. Seal according to directions in ABC's. Process jars 10 minutes in a boiling water bath.

GERTIE'S GARTER GARLIC DILLS
(Short Method, Indeed)

These dills are so named when 1/2 teaspoon of alum is omitted from the original recipe. It is enough to make anyone up tight and that Gertie wasn't. However, if you wish for a harder pickle, by all means use the alum. Be careful to use the stated amount, or you'll have a bitter pucker-pickle.

dill-size, 4-inch cucumbers
1 quart white vinegar
3 quarts purified water

1 cup pickling salt
1/2 teaspoon alum (optional)

Wash enough cucumbers to fill 6 quart jars. Mix vinegar, water, salt and alum, if using. Meanwhile to each quart jar add:

1 to 2 grape leaves, depending on size, or
   1 large horseradish leaf (If you use
   alum, omit these)

4 dill heads (2 on bottom, 2 on top)
1 hot red pepper
1 clove garlic, peeled and blanched

Pack the cucumbers, quartered if you wish, into sterilized jars. If whole, pierce the ends and middle of each cucumber to prevent mushy or hollow pickles. Pack to within 1/2 inch or so of the top of the jar. Add 2 dill heads on top. Pour boiling liquid over cucumbers to the top of the jar. Seal lids according to directions in ABC's. Let stand unshaken in a cool place for at least 30 days. The longer these age the better they become.
Makes 6 quarts

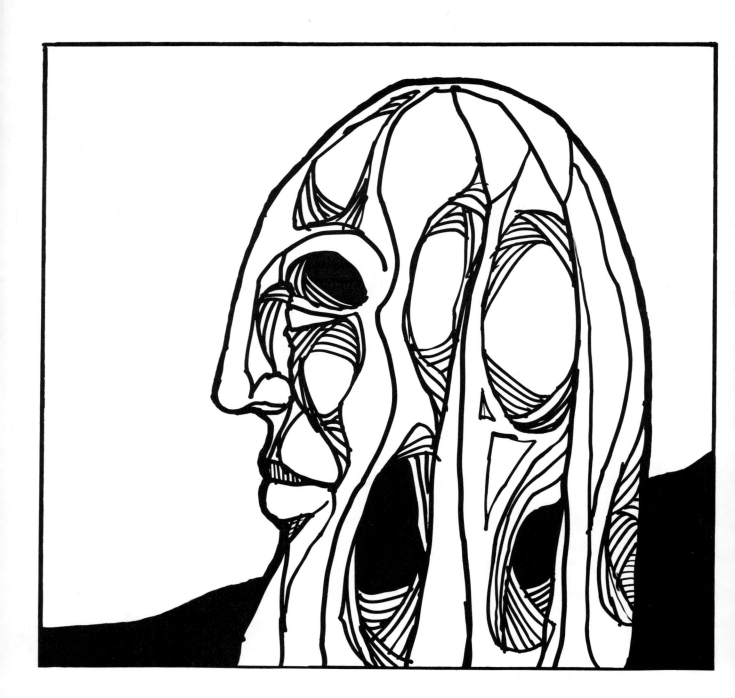

Everyman's pickles

PARISHA FARMER STARK'S
VERMONT FLINT PICKLES

50 medium cucumbers (about 6 pounds
    or 1 gallon)
brine of 2 quarts purified water to
    1/2 cup pickling salt
enough vinegar to cover pickles
    (about 2 quarts)
2 large onions, sliced

2 hot red peppers
2 heaping tablespoons crushed cinnamon
    stick
2 heaping tablespoons sliced horseradish
    root
1 tablespoon whole cloves
1 tablespoon whole allspice

Heat water and salt boiling hot. Pour over cucumbers to cover. Do this for 9 mornings, adding water and salt in same proportions if needed. On the 10th morning drain and wash well in cold purified water. Bring to a boil enough vinegar to cover pickles plus the onions, peppers and spices. Pack cucumbers in sterilized jars and pour hot vinegar solution over them. Ready for use when cold or you may can them immediately, following directions in ABC's.

41

ZUCCHINI PICKLE

4 pounds zucchini (about 9 cups, sliced)
1 pound small white onions
1/2 cup pickling salt
1 quart cider vinegar
2 cups sugar

2 teaspoons celery seed
2 teaspoons turmeric
2 teaspoons dry mustard
2 teaspoons mustard seed
2 cloves garlic, pressed

Cut zucchini unpeeled into thin slices, about 1/4 inch thick. Peel onions and slice thinly. Cover with purified water and add salt. Let stand 1 hour. Drain and rinse. Combine remaining ingredients. Bring to boil and pour over zucchini and onions. Let stand 1 hour. Return to heat and boil 2 to 3 minutes. Pour hot in sterilized jars. Seal according to instructions in ABC's.
Makes about 4 pints

SLICED CUCUMBER PICKLES

1 gallon medium-size cucumbers
boiling purified water

1 small handful pickling salt
cider vinegar

Put cucumbers into a stone crock and add enough boiling water to cover them completely. Add the salt, stir and cover; let stand overnight. Repeat this procedure 3 mornings. On the fourth morning scald enough vinegar to cover the pickles. Add:

1 piece alum as large as a walnut (1 scant
   teaspoon or less)
1 cup finely chopped horseradish root

1 teaspoon each dry mustard, ground
   cloves and ground cinnamon, in
   muslin bag

While this mixture is cooking slice the cucumbers into 1/2-inch pieces. Put into sterilized glass jars and pour the scalding vinegar over to cover. Seal according to directions in ABC's.

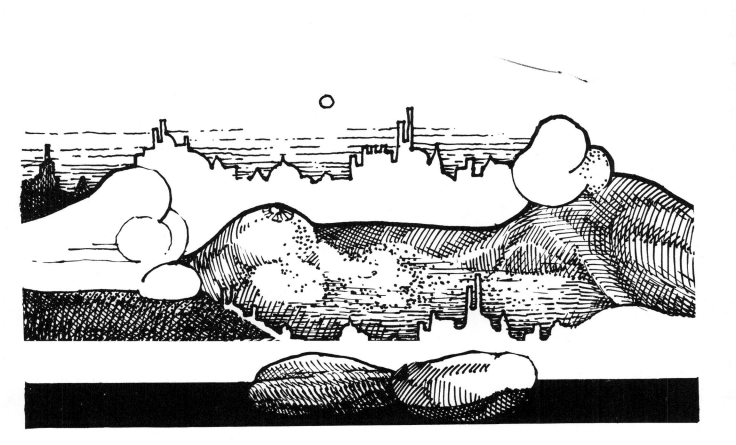

Fruit pickles

SWEET PICKLE FOR FRUIT

Most of the recipes for making a sweet pickle for fruit such as clingstone peaches, damson plums, cherries, apricots, etc. are so similar that we give the one which is the most successfully used.

to every quart of fruit allow:
1 cup white sugar
1 pint cider vinegar

2 tablespoons ground stick cinnamon
1 tablespoon whole cloves
1 tablespoon whole allspice

Carefully wash the fruit to be pickled. Damsons and other plums should be pricked with a needle and peaches rubbed with a coarse cloth to remove the fur. Put fruit in a large enameled pan. In a separate pan boil the vinegar and spices. Pour hot over the fruit to cover; let stand overnight. Then pour off vinegar, reboil and pour over fruit. Repeat this procedure 2 or 3 days in succession, adding more vinegar as needed to cover. With a slotted spoon put fruit carefully in sterilized jars. Do one jar at a time. Pour hot liquid on immediately, allowing about 1/4-inch headspace before sealing. Seal each jar as you go according to directions in ABC's.
If you wish to use the hot water bath process, follow the directions in ABC's. Never overdo it; generally about 10 minutes is adequate. If not careful, you will produce mush-fruit. You may well have to judge the timing for yourself by trial and error.
This is an adaptation from the *White House Cook Book* (1911).

CRAB APPLE PICKLES

Wash and remove the flower ends of the apples. Place 1 whole clove in the end but leave the stem on. Make a syrup of sugar and water in the proportions of 7 cups sugar to 2 quarts water; you will need enough to cover the apples well as they cook. Add a little red food coloring. Place the apples in a pot and simmer slowly in the syrup so each is partially cooked. Move them about to accomplish this but do not break the skins. Drain off syrup and pack apples carefully in sterilized jars. Add hot syrup to cover. Seal according to directions in ABC's.

CHERRY OLIVES

Fill 2 sterilized quart jars with carefully washed black cherries with stems. Put 1 tablespoon of pickling salt in each jar. Fill each jar with a mixture of 1 pint of cider vinegar to 1 cup purified water. Seal according to directions in ABC's.

PEAR PICKLE

for each quart small, sound pears:
1 pint cider vinegar
1 cup white sugar

1 teaspoon ground allspice
1 teaspoon ground cinnamon
1 teaspoon whole cloves

Remove blossom end of pears, wash and prick around the middle with a fork. Bring other ingredients to a boil. Add pears and boil until tender, about 10 minutes. With a slotted spoon put pears in sterilized jars one jar at a time. Pour boiling mixture over to top. Seal according to directions in ABC's.

JEAN HEITMAN'S SPICED PICKLED ORANGES

6 oranges
1 teaspoon pickling salt
2-1/2 cups white sugar
1/2 cup cider vinegar

1/4 cup corn syrup
24 whole cloves
12 2-inch pieces cinnamon stick

Rinse oranges and prick all around with a fork. Put in a saucepan and cover with purified water and salt. Boil 20 minutes. Drain. Add fresh purified water to cover and boil 20 minutes more. Drain. Cut oranges into quarters, remove seeds and put in a shallow baking dish just large enough to hold them.

In a saucepan combine the sugar, vinegar, corn syrup and 1/2 cup purified water. Bring to a boil, stirring constantly, until the sugar is dissolved. Add spices and boil 10 minutes. Pour syrup over orange quarters. Bake covered in a 275° oven for 1-1/2 hours, spooning syrup over oranges occasionally. Transfer the quarters with a slotted spoon to sterilized jars. Pour the hot syrup over and seal according to instructions in ABC's. Ready in about a month.

PICKLED CANTALOUPE

Peel a large unripe cantaloupe, remove seeds and cut into small pieces. Bring to boil enough Basic Spiced Vinegar, page 115, to cover fruit. Use sugar proportion you desire; either the medium-sour or the sweet would be best. Add melon and cook over a very low heat until the melon pieces are almost transparent. Remove cantaloupe to a bowl with a slotted spoon. Boil pickling liquid 10 minutes. Pour over melon. Cool completely; chill in refrigerator. Will be ready to eat immediately. Another great hors d'oeuvre.

GHERKINS

8 quarts 1-1/2- to 2-inch cucumbers
1 cup sugar
1 cup pickling salt
1/2 cup ground or prepared horseradish

3/4 teaspoon turmeric
1 tablespoon dry mustard
1 gallon cider vinegar

Wash cucumbers carefully, then dry. Boil other ingredients no more than 5 minutes. Pack cucumbers in sterilized jars and pour liquid over to cover. Seal according to directions in ABC's. Should be ready in about 4 weeks.
Makes 8 quarts

SWEET GHERKINS

Many of the old recipes for this delightful pickle call for a curing process which can take from 9 to 23 days. Because few modern cooks would take on such a time-consuming task, we have adapted one of the best recipes, which is from the U.S. Department of Agriculture and takes only 4 days. It produces good results, but a few tricks from some of the long, old recipes—you can teach a new pickle old tricks—greatly enhance the final product.

First, a note about horseradish. Never use the ordinary commercial kind which is additive-ridden, but horseradish packed in vinegar only. This is difficult to find, but in most areas there is usually some small concern or farmer smart enough to make it. (In the Spokane, Washington, valley there was such a farmer's smart wife who helped our family's fortunes greatly with her one-of-a-kind home-canned horse-radish.) If this variety is not available, try to find horseradish root. Blanch the root in boiling water 1 minute, cool, scrape and grate about 1 inch of it into each jar. The blanching is necessary to kill spoilage bacteria. The horseradish adds a tantalizingly piquant flavor and hardens the pickles. Instead, you can put a small horseradish leaf or cherry leaf into each jar for hardening, but they will not add much to the flavor. If you have difficulty obtaining these ingredients and are a home gardener, by all means raise your own horseradish.

50 to 60 cucumbers, 1-1/2 to 3 inches
   long (about 7 pounds)
1/2 cup pickling salt
8 cups white sugar
1-1/2 quarts cider vinegar
3/4 teaspoon turmeric

2 teaspoons celery seed
2 teaspoons whole mixed pickling spices
8 1-inch pieces stick cinnamon
2 teaspoons vanilla (if desired)
prepared horseradish or fresh
   horseradish root

FIRST DAY Morning: Wash cucumbers thoroughly, scrubbing with vegetable brush; stem ends may be left on if desired. Drain cucumbers; place in large container and cover with boiling purified water. Afternoon (6 to 8 hours later): Drain; cover with fresh purified boiling water.

SECOND DAY Morning: Drain; cover with fresh purified boiling water. Afternoon: Drain; add salt; cover with fresh purified boiling water.

THIRD DAY Morning: Drain; prick cucumbers on the ends and middle with an ice pick or knitting needle. Make syrup of 3 cups of the sugar and 3 cups of the vinegar; add turmeric and spices. Heat to boiling and pour over cucumbers. (Cucumbers will be partially covered at this point.) Afternoon: Drain syrup into pan; add 2 cups of the sugar and 2 cups of the vinegar to the syrup. Heat to boiling and pour over pickles.

FOURTH DAY Morning: Drain syrup into pan; add 2 cups of the sugar and 1 cup of the vinegar to syrup. Heat to boiling and pour over pickles. Afternoon: Drain syrup into pan; add remaining 1 cup sugar and the vanilla to syrup; heat to boiling. Just before packing the pickles into hot, sterilized pint jars, add 1/4 teaspoon prepared horseradish or about 1 inch horseradish root, grated (see directions above). Then pack pickles into the jars, and cover with boiling syrup to 1/2 inch of top of jar. Follow directions in ABC's for sealing.

Process for 5 minutes in a hot water bath. See ABC's for timing schedule as well as directions for processing and storage.

Makes 7 to 8 pints

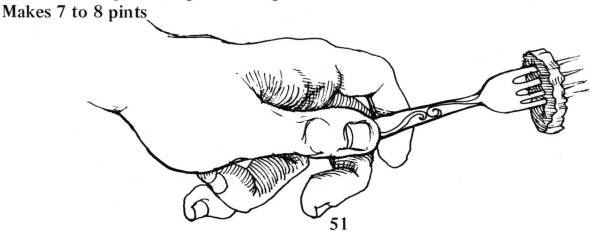

51

Hard
times
pickles

AUNT ELLA'S HARD TIMES PICKLES

For the home gardener this is a good way to put down cucumbers a few at a time. Wash the cucumbers carefully and put in a large crock or a half-barrel layers of cucumbers and rock salt alternately. Use enough salt to make sufficient brine to cover the cucumbers well. If uncertain about the brine, it should be strong enough to float an egg on top. Add no water. Cover with a cloth and place a heavy board over this so that the cucumbers are kept under the brine. Take off the cloth and rinse every time you put in more cucumbers because a scum will rise and settle on it. If your brine is sufficiently strong, these pickles will keep a year.

To prepare them for use, soak them in hot water and put in a warm place until they regain color. Then pour Basic Spiced Vinegar (see page 115) over them and let stand overnight. Pour that off and put on fresh spiced vinegar.

These pickles can be eaten soon after they have absorbed the spiced vinegar. If you wish, after you have poured off the overnight bath of spiced vinegar, you may can these using any of the recipes you want for sweet and sour, mustard pickles, etc.

BREAD AND BUTTER PICKLES

25 to 30 medium cucumbers
8 large white onions
2 large sweet peppers
1/2 cup pickling salt
5 cups cider vinegar

5 cups sugar
2 tablespoons mustard seed
1 teaspoon turmeric
1/2 teaspoon whole cloves

Wash cucumbers and slice thin. Chop onions and peppers and combine with the cucumbers. Sprinkle the 1/2 cup of salt over the cucumbers and cover with water. Let stand 3 hours. Drain and rinse.

Combine vinegar, sugar and spices in a large kettle. Bring to boil and add drained cucumber mixture. Heat but do not boil. Pack while hot into sterilized jars and seal according to directions in ABC's.

END OF THE SUMMER PICKLES

1 cup sliced cucumbers
1 cup chopped sweet peppers
1 cup chopped cabbage
1 cup sliced onions
1 cup chopped green tomatoes
brine of 2 quarts purified water to
   1/2 cup pickling salt
1 cup chopped carrots

1 cup green string beans cut in 1-inch
   pieces
2 tablespoons mustard seed
1 tablespoon celery seed
1 cup chopped celery
2 cups cider vinegar
2 cups white sugar
2 tablespoons turmeric
2 cloves pressed garlic

Soak cucumbers, peppers, cabbage, onions and tomatoes in brine overnight. Make sure the vegetables are covered. Drain and rinse. Cook the carrots and string beans in boiling water about 10 minutes. Drain well. Mix soaked and cooked vegetables with remaining ingredients and boil 10 minutes. Pack into sterilized quart jars and seal according to instructions in ABC's. Process in a hot water bath 5 minutes according to instructions in the ABC's.

POOR MAN'S PEPPER HASH

1 medium-size head cabbage
6 green bell peppers, seeded
6 medium-size onions

1 quart white or cider vinegar
1 cup sugar
2 tablespoons pickling salt

Coarsely grind vegetables together. Pour boiling water over; then drain and squeeze dry. Boil gently vinegar, sugar and salt. Place vegetable mixture in sterilized jars. Pour in the vinegar-sugar liquid to cover while hot. Seal according to directions in ABC's.

Icicle pickles

ICE WATER OR THE TITANIC PICKLE

cucumbers, celery and sliced onions
brine of 1 quart vinegar to 1 quart purified water,
1-1/2 cups sugar and 1/2 cup pickling salt

Soak cucumbers 3 hours in ice water; drain. Cut cucumbers in lengthwise slices and pack in sterilized glass jars, placing a stalk of celery in the center and sliced onions on top. Make sufficient brine to cover cucumbers; boil solution and pour over cucumbers. Seal according to directions in ABC's.

Jaded pickles

PICKLE OF RIPE AGED CUCUMBER

This is a French recipe and is the most excellent of all the high-flavored condiments; it is made by *sun-drying* thirty *old,* full-grown cucumbers, which have first been pared and split, had the seeds taken out, been salted and let stand twenty-four hours. The sun should be permitted to *dry,* not simply drain, them. When they are moderately dry, wash them with vinegar and place them in layers in a jar, alternating them with a layer of horseradish, mustard seed, garlic and onions for each layer of cucumbers. Boil in one quart of vinegar: 1 ounce [2 tablespoons] of race [root] ginger, half an ounce [1 tablespoon] of allspice and the same of turmeric; when cool pour this over the cucumbers, tie up [seal] tightly and set away. This pickle requires several months to mature it, but it is delicious when old, keeps admirably, and only a little is needed as a relish.

—*White House Cook Book* (1911)

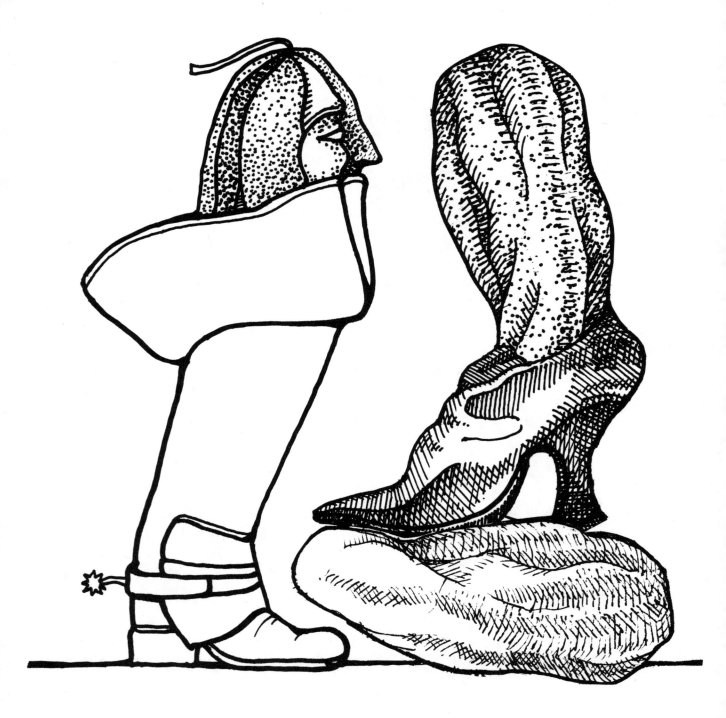

TURMERIC PICKLES

12 small onions
12 cucumbers, washed
brine of 1 cup pickling salt to 5 cups
   purified water
1 pint white or cider vinegar

1 cup sugar
1 teaspoon turmeric
1 teaspoon black pepper
1 teaspoon mustard seed
1 teaspoon celery seed

Slice the onions and cucumbers 1/4 inch thick. Cover in brine for 1 hour. Wash and drain. Combine vinegar with remaining ingredients. Add sliced onions and cucumbers and let simmer for 1 hour. Drain off liquid and pack cucumbers and onions into sterilized jars. Pour hot vinegar liquid over to cover and seal according to directions in ABC's.

CURRY PICKLES

24 medium-size cucumbers, cubed or
  thinly sliced (about 16 cups)
1/2 cup pickling salt
2 quarts purified water
1 teaspoon curry powder

2 cups cider vinegar
2-1/2 cups sugar
1/4 cup mustard seed
1 tablespoon celery seed
3 cloves pressed garlic

Wash cucumbers. Drain. Combine salt and purified water; add cucumbers. Let stand about 5 hours. Drain, rinse thoroughly in purified water. Mix remaining ingredients. Heat to boiling. Pour over cucumbers. Heat to boiling and put in sterilized jars. Seal according to instructions in ABC's.

CUCUMBER RAISIN PICKLES

6 medium-size cucumbers, sliced
  (about 4 cups)
brine of 1/2 cup pickling salt to
  2 quarts purified water
1 cup white vinegar

1 cup sugar
6 tablespoons raisins
1 tablespoon celery seed
1 tablespoon mustard seed

Soak cucumbers overnight in salt-water solution. Drain and rinse. Combine vinegar, sugar, raisins, celery and mustard seed. Heat to boiling. Add cucumbers and boil 10 minutes. Pack hot into sterilized jars and seal at once according to directions in ABC's.

Love pickles

RUBY'S SWEET PICKLES

small pickling cucumbers cut in 1/2-inch rounds
or larger cucumbers diced into 1/2-inch pieces
brine of 1 gallon water to 1 cup pickling salt
solution of 3 tablespoons alum to 1 gallon water

Be sure all water is purified as described in ABC's. Put cucumbers in a large crock or enameled pot. Cover the cucumbers with brine and soak for 24 hours. Drain, rinse and soak 12 hours in cold water. Drain. Make alum solution; heat until alum is thoroughly dissolved and liquid boils. Pour over the cucumbers to cover and let stand 24 hours. Drain. Cover cucumbers with boiling water; let stand 12 hours. Drain. Make a syrup to cover cucumbers in the proportions of:

3 quarts white or cider vinegar to 12 cups sugar and
2 tablespoons or more, as desired, whole pickling spices

Bring the syrup to a boil. Pour over the cucumbers and let stand 24 hours. Drain syrup off, add 3 cups sugar and heat to the point where the sugar is thoroughly dissolved. Pour over the cucumbers. Let stand 12 hours. Drain syrup off again, add 3/4 cup sugar and heat to the point where the sugar is dissolved. Pour over cucumbers. Pack while hot into sterilized jars, covering them with syrup. Seal according to directions in ABC's.

MAD MELODY PICKLES

2 quarts sliced small cucumbers
2 quarts thinly sliced large cucumbers
2 quarts small white onions
1/2 quart cut string beans
1/2 quart cut wax beans
2 large cauliflowers, flowerettes separated
4 hot red peppers
2 large green bell peppers, seeded and
    sliced
1/2 cup thinly shaved horseradish root
brine of 1-1/2 cups pickling salt to 2
    quarts purified water
1-1/2 gallons cider vinegar
5 pounds brown sugar
1/4 cup yellow mustard seed
1-1/2 teaspoons cayenne
2 tablespoons turmeric

Mix the cucumbers and vegetables and cover with the salt water. Let stand 24 hours; drain and rinse. Boil the vinegar, sugar and spices. Pour over pickles to cover; let stand 2 days. Pour in sterilized jars. Seal according to directions in ABC's.

SWEET DUTCH PICKLES

50 to 55 medium-size cucumbers (3 to 4 inches)
2 cups lime (calcium oxide)

Wash and slice cucumbers in 1/2-inch chunks. Put slices in a large enameled dishpan. Cover with purified water. Dissolve the lime in a little water separately. Pour this mixture over cucumbers. Let stand for 24 hours. After 24 hours drain off the lime solution. Wash thoroughly in clear water until *all* of the lime is gone. Cover with purified water and let stand 12 hours. Drain and wash again in purified water. Mix:

2 quarts cider vinegar
8 cups sugar
1 tablespoon whole cloves

3 teaspoons pickling salt
3 teaspoons celery seed
1 tablespoon mixed pickling spices

Heat this mixture until the sugar is thoroughly dissolved. Pour it over pickles and let stand overnight. Next morning boil 35 minutes or until cucumbers turn a clear color. Put hot in sterilized jars. Seal according to instructions in ABC's.
Makes 5 to 7 quarts

Mustard pickles

MUSTARD PICKLES

12 pounds small cucumbers (up to
   5 inches), sliced
brine of 2 quarts purified water to 1/2
   cup pickling salt
1 cup brown sugar, packed
1 cup white sugar

1/2 cup flour
1 teaspoon turmeric
1 quart white or cider vinegar
1 tablespoon dry mustard
2 tablespoons mustard seed
1 to 2 tablespoons celery seed

Cover the cucumbers in salt-water brine; soak 4 hours. Drain and rinse. Mix sugars, flour and turmeric. Blend into vinegar, then add dry mustard, mustard seed and celery seed. Cook slowly and stir until somewhat thickened. Add cucumbers and simmer 15 minutes, stirring frequently. Then pour hot into sterilized pint jars. Seal according to directions in ABC's.

AUNT DOLLY STARK DOWNEY'S MUSTARD PICKLES

1 quart green beans (about 1 pound), cut
1 quart cucumbers (about 3 to 4 medium), cut small
1 quart small pickling onions (about 24, small), peeled and sliced
2 large cucumbers, sliced
1 large cauliflower head, cut into flowerettes
3 red sweet peppers, seeded and cut up
brine of 1 cup pickling salt to 1 gallon purified water
1 quart white or cider vinegar

Soak each vegetable separately in brine to cover overnight. Scald each vegetable by boiling its brine and putting vegetable in for 1 minute. Drain off hot brine, rinse and mix vegetables together. Cover with vinegar, bring to boil slowly, stirring constantly; then remove from heat. Bring to boil slowly and stir:

1 quart white or cider vinegar
3 tablespoons dry mustard
3/4 cup brown sugar, packed

1/2 cup flour
1 tablespoon turmeric

Simmer this mixture until thickened; then pour the vinegar off the pickles and put the mustard mixture on them while hot. Put in sterilized jars, covering with mustard mixture. Seal according to directions in ABC's.

NASTURTIUM PODS PICKLED

From the Latin *nasus*, nose and *tortus* pp. of *torquere*, to twist. No doubt this name derives from the pungent odor of the plant. Take green nasturtium pods fresh from the vines. Put them in a solution of 6 tablespoons salt to 1 quart water for 3 days, changing brine daily. Drain. Put them in glass bottles and cover with cider vinegar. Keep closely corked. These are equal to capers with roast lamb. Ready to be eaten in a few days.

Onion & oil pickles

Great Uncle Perl Peregrine Stark,
inventor of the modern oil pickle
and onion pickle
Lost in the great pickle rush
to Saskatchewan

70

ONIONS PICKLED

Peel small white onions and cover them in a brine of 1 cup pickling salt to 7 cups purified water. Soak for 2 days, changing brine once. Drain them in a cloth, rinse and pack into sterilized bottles. Boil white vinegar with mace and black pepper to taste for 3 to 5 minutes. Let mixture cool, pour over onions to overflowing. Cork or seal according to directions in ABC's.

OILED ONIONS

4 quarts small white onions
  (about 96)
brine of 1 cup pickling salt to 7 cups
  purified water
2 quarts white vinegar

2 cups sugar
1/4 cup mixed pickling spices in
  muslin bag
1/4 cup olive oil

Scald the onions in boiling water for 2 minutes; drain. Cool in cold water and peel. Cover with brine and let stand overnight. The next day, drain and wash in cold water. Combine vinegar, sugar and spice bag in a pan and boil 3 to 5 minutes. Remove spices and add onions; let come just to a boil and pour at once almost to the top of sterilized jars. Pour in oil to fill and seal according to directions in ABC's. After the jars are sealed and cooled, shake gently to distribute the oil evenly.

Makes 4 quarts

OILED PICKLES

50 medium cucumbers
3 onions
1 cup pickling salt
2 quarts cold purified water
2 cups sugar
1 tablespoon peppercorns

2 tablespoons celery seed
2 tablespoons mustard seed
1/2 teaspoon turmeric
1/2 cup purified water
2 cups white or cider vinegar
1/2 cup olive oil

Slice cucumbers and onions very thin. Put them in the salt and cold water solution; let stand overnight or about 18 hours. Drain. Rinse well in cold water so that the cucumbers are not too salty. Boil sugar and spices with the 1/2 cup of water and vinegar about 1 minute. Add cucumbers, onions and oil and simmer. When the cucumbers change color, bring to boil. Pack boiling hot into sterilized jars and seal according to directions in ABC's.
Makes about 7 quarts

SIMPLY OILED PICKLES

4 quarts sliced cucumbers (about 50 medium)
brine of 1 cup pickling salt to 9 cups purified water
1/2 teaspoon whole cloves
1/2 teaspoon whole allspice
1/2 teaspoon celery seed

2 teaspoons ground cinnamon
1/2 cup olive oil
1/2 cup sugar
1/2 cup mustard seed
12 small onions
white or cider vinegar

Cover sliced cucumbers with boiling water. When cold, drain and cover with brine. Let stand overnight; drain and rinse next morning. Mix all ingredients with enough cold vinegar to cover the pickles. Pour into sterilized jars and seal according to directions in ABC's.

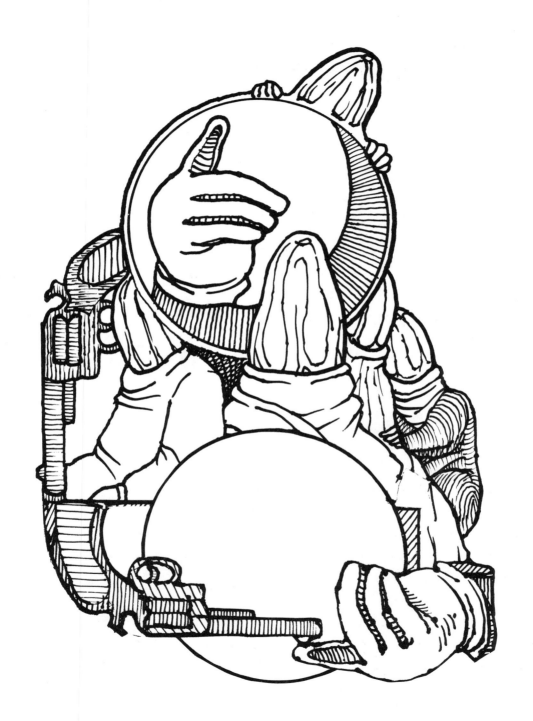

PICKLED GREEN PEPPERS

12 large green bell peppers
brine of 1 cup pickling salt to 5 cups
   purified water
white or cider vinegar
1 small piece alum (1/8 to 1/4 teaspoon)

2 hard heads white cabbage
pickling salt to taste
1 cup white mustard seed
Spiced Vinegar (see page 116)

Wash peppers and extract the seeds by cutting a slit in the sides so as to leave them whole. Make a brine strong enough to float an egg (approximately in the above proportions). Pour over the peppers to cover; let stand 24 hours. Take them out of the brine and soak them in purified water to cover for a day and a night. Drain.
Scald some vinegar, put in the small piece alum. Pour over the peppers to cover and let stand 3 days.
Chop cabbage fine, season slightly with pickling salt and add the cup of mustard seed. Mix well. Stuff the peppers hard and full. Stitch them up with strong white thread. Put in a stone jar and pour a mixture of scalding hot vinegar over them to cover. Put in sterilized jars and seal according to directions in ABC's. The peppers may also be placed in a cool place in a tightly covered stone jar, in case you wish to use a large quantity soon.

SIMPLE PICKLED PEPPERS

Wash green and red sweet peppers; remove seeds and tops. Cut in desired shapes, strips or small pieces. Make a solution in the following proportions:

1 pint white or cider vinegar
1/4 cup purified water

2 cups sugar
2 tablespoons pickling salt

Heat enough solution to cover peppers. Taste and add more salt if desired. Put in peppers; simmer until peppers turn color. Pour hot into sterilized jars. Seal according to directions in ABC's.

GREEN PEPPER MANGOES

This kind of "mango" is not the tropical fruit, but a pickled stuffed sweet pepper. Select both red and green sweet peppers. With a sharp knife remove the tops and take out the seeds. Soak tops and bottoms overnight in a brine of 1 cup pickling salt to 7 cups purified water to cover. Drain and rinse. Fill with chopped cabbage and green tomatoes seasoned with salt, mustard seed and ground cloves. Sew on the tops; pack into sterilized jars.

Combine sufficient vinegar to cover the peppers with 1 cup packed brown sugar. Boil 3 to 5 minutes and pour hot over the mangoes. Let stand 1 day. Next morning, drain liquid and reboil. Add vinegar if necessary. Pour hot over mangoes to cover. Do this 3 mornings, the last day placing the mangoes in sterilized jars filled with the hot liquid. Seal according to directions in ABC's.

PICKLED HOT YELLOW PEPPERS

Wash hot yellow peppers, drain and pack into sterilized jars. If desired, put a clove of garlic in the bottom of each jar. Make a solution in the proportions of:

1 pint white vinegar   1/2 cup sugar
1 pint purified water   2 tablespoons pickling salt

Boil mixture about 3 minutes. Pour hot over peppers to cover. Seal according to directions in ABC's.

Quick pickles

LAZY HOUSEWIFE'S PICKLES

small cucumbers
pickling solution of 1 gallon white or
   cider vinegar to

1 cup sugar
1 cup pickling salt
1 cup dry mustard

Pack small cucumbers in sterilized jars. Prepare pickling solution in proportions shown above but do not heat. Cover cucumbers with solution. Seal jars according to directions in ABC's. Ready in 2 to 3 months.

FRESH SOUR CUCUMBER SLICES

Use medium-sized cucumbers. Peel and slice very thin. Sprinkle each gallon of slices with 1 cup of pickling salt. Let stand for 12 hours. Drain and rinse. Put the slices in sterilized glass jars and cover with pure, cold cider vinegar. Seal according to directions in ABC's. Store 1 month before use.

THE LAZIEST SWEET DILL PICKLES IN TOWN

Just take your aged, whole dill pickles. Drain, reserving liquid and slice crosswise into chunks about 1/4 inch wide. Pour 1 cup sugar into the old liquid. Put the pickles in your jar and cover. Shake until the sugar has dissolved. Put in the refrigerator and let stand a week or two.

QUICKIE DILL PICKLES

Wash the cucumbers and let stand in cold water a few hours. Drain, rinse and pack into sterilized jars. For each 1/2 gallon of cucumbers, make a solution of:

6 stalks dill
1/2 cup white or cider vinegar

3 tablespoons pickling salt
1 hot red pepper (or to taste)

Pour in jars. Fill with cold boiled water. Seal according to directions in ABC's. Ready to use in 1 month.

Relishes & sauces

CHOW-CHOW

1 quart cucumbers (about 6, not over 2 inches long), peeled and chopped
2 quarts very small white onions (about 24 medium)
2 quarts tender string beans (about 2 pounds), cut in halves
3 quarts green tomatoes (about 15), coarsely chopped
2 heads cauliflower, cut into small pieces
2 heads white cabbage, finely chopped
pickling salt to taste

Put vegetables in a stone jar or crock and mix together, sprinkling in salt sparingly. Let this mixture stand for 24 hours; then drain off all the brine and rinse. Put vegetables in a kettle and add:

2 tablespoons turmeric
6 sweet red peppers, coarsely chopped
1/4 cup mustard seed
2 tablespoons celery seed
2 tablespoons whole allspice

2 tablespoons whole cloves
1 cup sugar
2/3 cup dry mustard
enough cider vinegar to cover the mixture well

Cover tightly and simmer until vegetables seem tender. Watch and stir often. Put hot into sterilized bottles or glass jars and seal according to directions in ABC's. As it ages, the flavor improves.

SALEM SUCCOTASH RELISH

"Oh, what a witch's brew."
—Macbeth

12 ears sweet corn (Or, if you should want to make this in the winter, use about 3 cups frozen or canned kernel corn.)

4 cups chopped cabbage (about 1 pound)
3 sweet green peppers, seeded
3 sweet red peppers, seeded
3 hot red peppers, or 1 tablespoon dried crushed red pepper pods

Cut the kernels from the corn. Put the other ingredients through food chopper with a coarse blade. Mix the following:

2 teaspoons dry mustard
1 tablespoon celery seed
1 tablespoon mustard seed
1-1/4 teaspoons turmeric

2 cups sugar
1/2 cup flour
1-1/2 teaspoons pickling salt
1 quart white or cider vinegar

Add corn and chopped vegetables. Cook 10 minutes. Pour hot into sterilized jars and seal according to directions in ABC's.

TOMATO RELISH

20 ripe tomatoes
3 small onions, chopped fine
3 green bell peppers, chopped fine
1/4 cup pickling salt

1 cup brown sugar, packed
1 cup chopped celery
1-1/2 pints white or cider vinegar
ground cinnamon to taste
2 tablespoons white mustard seed

Cut tomatoes small, drain off excess liquid and discard. Mix all ingredients together. Pour uncooked into sterilized jars and seal according to directions in ABC's.

Peregrine Pickle
in his relish days

HOT DOG RELISH

2 cups coarsely chopped onions (about 3 large)
2 cups coarsely chopped cabbage (about 1/4 head)
6 green bell peppers, seeded and cut up
3 sweet red peppers, seeded and cut up
1 quart quartered tomatoes (about 5 medium)
1/4 cup pickling salt

3 cups sugar
1 quart white or cider vinegar
1 cup purified water
3/4 teaspoon turmeric
1 tablespoon dry mustard
1 tablespoon mustard seed
1/2 tablespoon celery seed
1 quart or less to taste dill pickles
1 quart or less to taste sweet pickles

Put vegetables through food chopper with coarse blade. Sprinkle them with salt and let stand overnight; rinse and drain. Combine remaining ingredients, except the dill and sweet pickles, and pour over vegetables. Heat to boil and simmer for 3 minutes. Chop the amount of dill and sweet pickles desired and add to mixture just before it is poured hot into sterilized jars. If you wish, add some of the liquids from dill and sweet pickle jars. Seal according to directions in ABC's.
Makes about 4 to 5 pints

A DIXIE MELODY RELISH

4 quarts cored and chopped green tomatoes (about 32 medium)
2 quarts peeled, cored and chopped ripe tomatoes (about 12 large)
2 quarts chopped cabbage (about 1 large head
6 cups chopped onion (about 12 medium)
4 cups chopped celery (about 1 pound)
2 cups chopped green bell peppers (about 4 medium)
2 cups chopped sweet red peppers (about 4 medium)

2 cups chopped cucumbers (about 2 to 3 large)
1 cup pickling salt
4 quarts white or cider vinegar
8 cups brown sugar, packed
2 tablespoons celery seed
2 tablespoons mustard seed
2 tablespoons ground cinnamon
2 tablespoons ground nutmeg
2 teaspoons ground ginger
1 teaspoon ground cloves
4 cloves garlic, pressed

Mix vegetables; thoroughly sprinkle with salt. Let stand about 16 hours in a cool place. Drain and rinse well. Mix vinegar, sugar and spices; simmer 10 minutes. Add vegetables and simmer 30 minutes. Bring to boil.

Pack vegetables boiling hot into sterilized jars, leaving about 1/8-inch headspace. Cover with vinegar mixture and seal according to directions in ABC's.

To make a curry relish from this recipe simply add 4 cups raisins and 4 teaspoons curry powder when the vegetable mix is added to the pickling solution.

Peregrine Wilkes Booth,
Southern Pickle sympathizer,
lost in Texas
after the Civil War

CHERRY RELISH

3 cups pitted red cherries
1-1/2 cups seedless raisins
1-1/2 teaspoons ground cinnamon
1/2 teaspoon ground cloves

1 cup honey
1 cup white sugar
1 cup brown sugar, packed
1-1/2 cups white or cider vinegar
1-1/2 cups chopped pecan meats

Combine all ingredients except the pecans and cook slowly 1 hour. Add pecans and cook 3 minutes. Pour hot into sterilized jars; seal as directed in ABC's.

PICCALILLI

1 head cabbage
6 sweet red peppers, seeded
6 green bell peppers, seeded
5 large onions
6 green tomatoes
2 tablespoons pickling salt

2-1/2 cups sugar
3 cups white or cider vinegar
3 tablespoons mustard seed
2 tablespoons celery seed
1/2 teaspoon turmeric

Put cabbage, peppers, onions and tomatoes through food chopper with a coarse blade. Add salt and let stand overnight. Drain fairly dry. Mix in the rest of the ingredients; boil about 20 minutes. Pour hot into sterilized jars and seal according to directions in ABC's.

SCHUBERT'S UNCOOKED RELISH SYMPHONY

2 pints seeded and chopped sweet red peppers (about 10 large)
2 pints seeded and chopped sweet green peppers (about 10 large)
2 quarts chopped cabbage (about 1 medium-large head)
2 pints chopped white onions (about 12 medium-small)

4 teaspoons celery seed
4 pounds sugar
1/2 cup mustard seed

2 quarts white or cider vinegar
3 to 4 hot red peppers
10 tablespoons pickling salt

Put each vegetable through food chopper with a coarse blade. Drain and discard liquid. Mix all ingredients and let stand overnight. In morning pack into sterilized jars and seal according to directions in ABC's.

AUNT NELLIE STARK MACDONALD'S
CUCUMBER RELISH

4 cucumbers, peeled and chopped
2 pints finely chopped celery (about
   a bunch)
2 tablespoons pickling salt
1 pint white or cider vinegar
1/2 cup sugar

few grains cayenne
1/4 cup grated horseradish root or
   unadulterated prepared horseradish
1/4 cup finely chopped onion
1/4 cup finely chopped green bell pepper
2 teaspoons black pepper

Combine cucumbers with celery and sprinkle with salt. Place in a cheesecloth bag and let drain overnight. Rinse well, drain and add the other ingredients. Pour uncooked into sterilized jars and seal according to directions in ABC's. This is excellent with fish and can be used in a few weeks.

ZUCCHINI RELISH

10 zucchini
4 onions
2 green bell peppers, seeded
2 sweet red peppers, seeded
1/2 cup pickling salt
2-1/2 cups white or cider vinegar

4-1/2 cups sugar
2 tablespoons cornstarch
1 teaspoon turmeric
1 teaspoon ground nutmeg or curry
   powder
1 teaspoon celery salt
1/2 teaspoon black pepper

Put the zucchini, onions and peppers through a food chopper with a coarse blade. Sprinkle 1/2 cup of salt over them. Let stand overnight; drain and rinse. Add remaining ingredients. Bring to a boil; simmer 10 minutes. Pour hot into sterilized jars and seal according to directions in ABC's.

GRANDMA STARK GEE'S PEPPER HASH

1 medium-sized head cabbage, shredded
6 sweet green peppers,
  seeded and chopped
6 sweet red peppers,
  seeded and chopped

6 medium-sized onions, chopped
1 quart white or cider vinegar
1 cup sugar
2 tablespoons pickling salt

Pour boiling water over cabbage, peppers and onions to cover. Drain and squeeze dry. Put vegetables in the vinegar, sugar and salt solution and bring to a boil. Pour hot into sterilized jars and seal according to directions in ABC's.

RED PEPPER RELISH

14 to 16 sweet red peppers, finely
   chopped
2 tablespoons pickling salt

6 cups sugar
1 quart white or cider vinegar
1/2 teaspoon ground nutmeg

Mix peppers and salt; let stand 4 hours. Rinse and drain. Add sugar, vinegar and nutmeg; cook about 45 minutes, stirring frequently, until thick. Pour boiling hot into sterilized jars, leaving about 1/8-inch headspace. Seal according to directions in ABC's. A marvelous sweet-sour companion with meats.

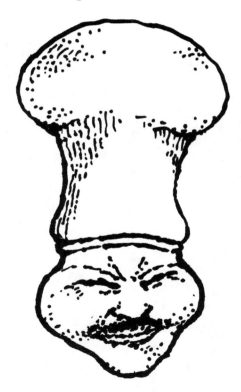

BEET OR RED RELISH

1 quart chopped cooked beets (about
  1 pound)
1 quart chopped cabbage (about
  1 small head)
1 cup chopped onions
1 cup chopped sweet red peppers
  (about 2 medium)

1 cup chopped celery
pinch of cayenne
1 tablespoon pickling salt
1 tablespoon prepared horseradish
1-1/2 cups sugar
3 cups white or cider vinegar

Mix all ingredients. Simmer 10 minutes, then bring to a boil. Pack boiling hot into sterilized 1/2-pint jars, leaving about 1/8-inch headspace. Seal according to directions in ABC's.
Makes about 3 half-pints

BEET RELISH

1 cup chopped, cold cooked beets
3 tablespoons grated horseradish root
  (prepared horseradish may be substituted to taste)

2 tablespoons lemon juice
1 teaspoon table salt

Mix in order named. Use fresh. Delicious served with cold meat or fish.

NEW ENGLAND CHILI SAUCE

40 large tomatoes, peeled and quartered
2 to 3 hot red peppers, chopped
6 sweet green or red peppers, seeded
   and chopped
2 cups sugar
1 pint cider vinegar

2-1/2 tablespoons pickling salt
1 tablespoon ground ginger
1 tablespoon ground cinnamon
1-1/2 teaspoons ground allspice
1-1/2 teaspoons ground nutmeg
1-1/2 teaspoons celery seed

Simmer tomatoes 4 to 5 hours in water to cover; drain slowly and throw away excess juice. Add all other ingredients. Let simmer slowly until thickened. Pour hot into sterilized jars, leaving 1/8-inch headspace; seal according to directions in ABC's. Process in a hot water bath for 15 minutes.
This is a basic recipe which can be infinitely varied. If you like a hotter sauce, merely add a couple more hot red peppers.
Makes 18 pints

CHILI SAUCE

24 tomatoes, peeled and quartered
6 onions, chopped
3 green bell peppers, seeded and chopped
3 hot red peppers, chopped
1 cup brown sugar, packed
5 cups white or cider vinegar

3 tablespoons pickling salt
1 teaspoon mustard seed
1 teaspoon whole cloves
1 teaspoon whole allspice
1 teaspoon ground cinnamon

Mix vegetables, sugar and vinegar. Tie spices in a bag. Boil until thick. Remove bag and pour hot into sterilized jars. Seal according to directions in ABC's.
Makes 4-1/2 pints

HORSERADISH

Wash horseradish roots well in hot water. Scrape off the skin. Grate or mince into a bowl and cover with a mixture in the proportions of 1 pint white vinegar to 1 teaspoon pickling salt. Seal in small sterilized jars according to directions in ABC's. Store in the refrigerator; ready to use in a week or so.

RUBY'S RHUBARB SAUCE

8 pints chopped rhubarb (about 1 to
  2 pounds)
1 cup chopped onion
3 cups chopped raisins
7 cups brown sugar, packed
1 cup white or cider vinegar

2 teaspoons salt
2 teaspoons grated fresh ginger root
2 teaspoons ground cinnamon
2 teaspoons whole allspice
2 teaspoons ground nutmeg

Mix rhubarb, onion, raisins, sugar and vinegar. Carefully boil, stirring from time to time, until thickened. Put spices in a bag and boil another 5 minutes. Remove spices and pour boiling hot into jars. Seal. Excellent with meats.
Makes about 15 pints

If you follow the canning method below, you can take advantage of cheap rhubarb in the summer or the excess from your own garden, and make this sauce the year around. Simply cut raw rhubarb to fit in sterilized quart jars. Fill with *cold* purified water. Heat lids. Seal according to directions in ABC's.

LUCREZIA BORGIA'S LEMON DELIGHT

juice and grated peel of 12 large lemons
1 onion, chopped fine
2 tablespoons grated fresh horseradish
1/4 cup white mustard seed
1 tablespoon white pepper
1 tablespoon turmeric

1 teaspoon ground cloves
1 teaspoon mace
few grains cayenne
2 tablespoons sugar
2 tablespoons pickling salt

Mix all ingredients together. Let stand in a cool place at least 3 hours. Bring to boil and cook 30 minutes or until thickened. Pour into a stone crock or large jar, cover tightly and let stand 2 weeks, stirring well every day. Strain through a doubled cheesecloth bag and pour strained liquid into hot, sterilized bottles. Seal according to directions in ABC's. Marvelous with fish.
Makes 2 pints

BORDEAUX SAUCE

1 gallon finely chopped cabbage (about 16 cups or 4 pounds)
2 quarts green tomatoes (about 5 large), sliced
10 medium onions, sliced
1/2 bunch celery, cut fine
1 tablespoon ground cloves

1 tablespoon whole allspice
1 tablespoon turmeric
black pepper to taste
1/8 pound white mustard seed (about 1/3 cup)
1 pound sugar
1/2 cup pickling salt
2 quarts cider vinegar

Mix all ingredients well. Boil 15 minutes. Pour hot into sterilized jars and seal according to directions in ABC's.

Sauerkraut

SAUERKRAUT

Sauerkraut means much more than sour cabbage. It is a great source of vitamin C and minerals which for centuries kept the scourge of scurvy away from peasants and nobles alike, who ate it although they didn't know why. It was in comparatively recent times that its powers were realized. It was and is easily made, if a few simple rules are observed.

Also, few utensils are needed. You can get by with a sharp knife, a large enameled or aluminum pan, a stone crock or glass jar and a bottle. But if you are going to make it in quantity, a good kraut cutting board with adjustable blades is recommended. (This is also perfect for making scalloped potatoes and the like.) They are inexpensive and can be found in any good hardware store.

The cardinal requirement in making kraut is to cure it at the right temperature. The best quality kraut is made at a temperature below 60°, which requires at least a month of fermentation. It may be cured at a higher temperature, and some authorities opt for this method because it is quicker. However, the kraut does not have the same color, texture and crispness when prepared this way. When properly done it has no white spots, but is firm and fetchingly yellow-white.

The next requirement is to use the proper kind of salt and the proper proportion. Use pickling salt, *never* table salt. The following is a good gauge for the proportion of salt to cabbage:

2 teaspoons salt for 1 pound cabbage

1/2 pound salt for 20 pounds cabbage

Mistakes that are made with kraut are:

- Not packing it firmly in the crock, so that air pockets remain.
- Not keeping it covered with brine at all times. If there is too much evaporation, more water and salt can always be added.
- Too weak a brine or an uneven distribution of salt.
- Not skimming off the scum faithfully, but more of this requirement later.
- Letting it ferment past its prime.

If these mistakes are made, you will get a soft, pinkish or dark kraut. Now to the alchemy of it all.

Select large, heavy and firm cabbage. Let it stand for a day to wilt. This will soften the leaves so that they will not break into too small pieces when you shred them. Remove outside leaves, quarter heads and core. Slice or shred to the desired thickness; about the thickness of a dime (and certainly worth more than one these days) is about right.

Put about 5 pounds of the shredded cabbage into a large enameled or aluminum pan. Sprinkle with 1/4 cup of salt, mix thoroughly and then pack into the crock. If you like, at this point you may add a cup of tart apples, cut very fine.

Take a large bottle, wooden tamper or rolling pin and pound down the cabbage until you see the juices begin to form and cover the cabbage. Repeat this process for each 5 pounds.

Whatever the size of your crock, you should leave a space of at least 2 inches at the top. (A 2-gallon crock holds about 15 pounds of cabbage, for example.) Cover the kraut with a fitted square of cloth, then a board (not pine) or a plate and weigh this down with a stone or a bottle filled with water so that the brine comes over the cloth.

When the fermentation begins after about a week, pick up the cloth by its edges to remove the scum. Wash the cloth, the board and the weight daily; also the sides of the crock if need be. Also make *certain* the kraut is covered with brine. If there is evaporation after a few weeks, you can add 1/4 cup of salt to a quart of water to pour over the kraut.

When the fermentation has ceased, you'll see no more frothy bubbles or scum on the cloth. The kraut is ready for preserving and eating. Actually, after the first week or so it makes good eating raw as well, because it resembles the cabbage both the Chinese and Japanese favor.

If you intend to use much of it soon, merely cover it in smaller containers and put in the refrigerator. If you intend to use it only from time to time, you can pour a good quality of hot paraffin over the surface of the crock to seal. Later you can use what you wish and replace the paraffin, after remelting it.

However, for long-term storage the following canning method is recommended: Heat kraut to simmering, about 180°; pack it very hard into hot jars and add sufficient kraut juice or a weak brine (2 tablespoons of salt to a quart of water) to cover. Leave about a 1/2-inch headspace. Seal according to directions in ABC's. Process in a boiling water bath, 25 minutes for pints, 30 minutes for quarts. To do this use a large pot with a rack on the bottom so that the jars will not get too hot and crack. The jars should be completely covered with boiling water.

If you wish, before completely filling the jars, you may mix in caraway seed or cardamom. In case you like garlic kraut, similar to Polish kraut, blanch cloves of garlic; that is, quickly put them in boiling water and pluck them out. Then put through a sterilized press and mix in to taste. The blanching is necessary because garlic often carries bacteria which could spoil the kraut.

SAUERKRAUT IN JARS

This is a quick, simple way of making sauerkraut in small quantities, especially convenient for the cook when he or she finds cabbage a bargain, but doesn't have time for the long method of krauting. It takes about 2 pounds of cabbage to fill a quart jar. Press shredded cabbage into a quart jar until half full, add 1 teaspoon of pickling salt. Make certain this is well packed. Press in more cabbage to the curve of the jar. Add 1 teaspoon of pickling salt. Fill jar with cold purified water to overflowing. Screw on lid loosely, for air must escape during the fermentation. Let stand at room temperature for 9 days. Fill jar up each day with water as it evaporates. At the end of this time, when the fermentation is finished, screw the cover tight. It is not necessary, but you may process the jars in a boiling water bath (as directed in the preceding) if you wish. Can be eaten immediately.

Tomato pickles

JOLLY GREEN TOMATO PICKLES

10 pounds small green tomatoes
8 medium onions
2 quarts purified water

1/2 cup pickling salt
1 cup white or cider vinegar
3 cups purified water

Slice tomatoes and onions 1/4 inch thick. Make brine of 2 quarts water and salt. Pour over the slices. (If not enough to cover, add more water and salt in the same proportions.) Let stand overnight. Drain and rinse.

Pour vinegar and 3 cups water over tomatoes and onions. Simmer slowly until tomatoes look rather transparent and have turned a light color. Make a syrup of:

1 quart white or cider vinegar
3 cups brown sugar, packed

1 tablespoon celery seed
1 tablespoon whole mixed pickling
    spices in muslin bag

Boil syrup until spices have permeated it to taste. With a slotted spoon, put pickles in sterilized jars. Pour syrup over to top of jars. Seal each jar as you go according to directions in ABC's.

GREEN TOMATO DILL PICKLES

Select small green tomatoes. Use the same recipe as in Gertie's Garter Garlic Dills (page 39) for the method and pickling solution. Leave out the garlic if you wish.

MARY LOUISE'S
FIRE AND ICE TOMATOES

3/4 cup white or cider vinegar
1-1/2 teaspoons celery seed
1-1/2 teaspoons mustard seed
1/2 teaspoon table salt
4-1/2 teaspoons sugar

1/8 teaspoon cayenne
1/8 teaspoon black pepper
6 tomatoes, quartered
1 green pepper, seeded and sliced
1 medium onion, sliced

Combine vinegar with spices and heat. Pour over the vegetables while hot. Chill. Should be eaten immediately.

TOMATO CHUNKS

for each quart barely ripe tomatoes:
3/4 cup white or cider vinegar
1/2 cup brown sugar, packed
1-1/2 teaspoons pickling salt

1 teaspoon whole mixed pickling spices,
   in muslin bag
1/2 teaspoon ground ginger
1/4 teaspoon grated nutmeg

Remove stem ends of tomatoes and cut into 1-inch chunks. Make a syrup of the remaining ingredients and boil for 5 minutes. Add tomato chunks and boil another 5 minutes. Remove spice bag. Pour boiling hot into sterilized jars and seal at once according to directions in ABC's.

Pressed garlic and minced onion may be added during the last 5-minute boiling if desired. Great with a Chinese dinner.

CHEKHOV'S CHERRY TOMATO ORCHARD PICKLES

4 pounds small green cherry tomatoes
4 dill heads
3 small cloves garlic, pressed
1 tablespoon grated horseradish root, or
   2 tablespoons unadulterated prepared
   horseradish
1 small onion, minced

2 teaspoons mustard seed
2 teaspoons mixed pickling spices
1 small hot red pepper
1 pint white vinegar
2 teaspoons pickling salt
4 cups purified water

Remove tomato stems and discard. Wash and pack in sterilized quart jars. Bring vinegar and spices to boil, no more than 1 minute. Pour over tomatoes, filling jar to the very top. Seal according to directions in ABC's.

Makes about 2 quarts

Utterly outré recipes

EAST INDIA PICKLE

Lay in a strong brine [see directions in ABC's] for two weeks, or until convenient to use them, small cucumbers, very small common white onions, snap beans, gherkins, hard white cabbage quartered, plums, peaches, pears, lemons, green tomatoes and anything else you may wish. When ready, take them out of the brine and simmer in pure water until tender enough to stick a straw through—if too salty, soak in clear water; drain thoroughly and lay them in vinegar in which is dissolved one ounce [2 tablespoons] of turmeric to the gallon. For five gallons of pickle, take two ounces [4 tablespoons] of mace, two ounces of cloves, two of cinnamon, two of allspice, two of celery seed, a quarter of a pound of white race ginger [race means root], cracked fine, half a pound of white mustard seed, half a pint of small red peppers, quarter of a pound of grated horseradish, half a pint of flour mustard [powdered], two ounces [4 tablespoons] of turmeric, half a pint of garlic, if you like; soak in two gallons of cider vinegar for two weeks, stirring daily. After the pickles have lain in the turmeric vinegar for a week, take them out and put in jars or casks, one layer of pickle and one of spice out of the vinegar, till all is used. If the turmeric vinegar is still good and strong, add it and the spiced vinegar. If the turmeric vinegar be much diluted, do not use it, but add enough fresh to the spiced to cover the pickles; put it on the fire with a pound of brown sugar to each gallon; when boiling pour over the pickle. Repeat this two or three times as your taste may direct.

—*White House Cook Book* (1911)

Note: If you wish to seal this pickle, use sterilized jars. Put in pickle. Pour over liquid boiling hot and seal according to the directions given in the ABC's. Process in a hot water bath, if you wish, for 5 minutes following the directions in the ABC's. In a crock these pickles will keep well if properly covered with the vinegar and spice liquid, for a long time if stored in a cool place. If you wish, place crock in the refrigerator. Use your imagination in making this recipe for it comes out tasting very much like an expensive chutney.

PICKLED EGGS

Pickled eggs are very easily prepared and most excellent as an accompaniment for cold meats. Boil quite hard three dozen eggs, drop in cold water and remove the shells, and pack them when entirely cold in a wide-mouthed jar, large enough to let them in or out without breaking. Take as much vinegar as you think will cover them entirely and boil in it white pepper, allspice, a little root ginger; pack them in stone or wide-mouthed glass jars, occasionally putting in a tablespoon of white and black mustard seed mixed, a small piece of race [root] ginger, garlic, if liked, horseradish ungrated, whole cloves and a very little allspice. Slice two or three green peppers and add in very small quantities. Pour over the vinegar cold. They will be fit for use in eight or ten days. Store in a cool place [or in the refrigerator].

—*White House Cook Book* (1911)

PICKLED WALNUTS

Take one hundred walnuts, picked about midsummer while the shells are still in the green stage, before the shells have formed, soft enough to allow a needle to pass through them, lay them in water with a good handful of salt for two days then change to fresh water and another handful of salt for three days; then drain, and lay them on some clean straw or a sieve, in the sun until quite black and wrinkled; afterwards put into a clean, dry glass bottle or jar a quarter of an ounce of allspice, quarter of an ounce of mace, quarter of an ounce of ginger, half a pint of mustard seed and half an ounce of peppercorns; these to be mixed in layers with the walnuts until your walnuts are all used. Then pour over them boiling vinegar to cover them. Bottle and seal. Ready for use in two months.

—*Universal Cookery Book* (1894)

Note: This recipe can be turned into walnut catsup by boiling for 1 hour. Let mixture become cold before bottling and sealing.

MUSKMELON MANGO

Take an unripe muskmelon (cantaloupe), just before it begins to ripe the better, wash it in cold water, cut out a small section on the side most rounded and scoop out the seeds and soft pulp; scrape off the soft matter from the section and preserve it for the "lid." Pare off the rind carefully, so as to leave all of the tender portion of the shell. Put a tablespoon pure salt in the cavity, place the muskmelon in a bowl and pour hot water over and in it, and let it remain eight to twelve hours. Then have your filling—generally of finely chopped cabbage but it is a matter of taste. Beet stems, tender string beans, etc. can be used. Three or four small slices of green pepper, lining the shell will spice it; white mustard seed or any other condiment is good. A preferable way is to tie up in a small piece of muslin the spice you desire and boil them in the vinegar in which you pickle it.

The hot water and salt make the shell soft and pliable and render the "stuffing" process easy. When filled, stitch the segment cut out of it carefully over the aperture.

A common practice is to "disembowel" a large red or green pepper and fill it with chopped vegetables. The advantage in the melon is that the rind is better than the best cucumber pickle.

—Universal Cookery Book (1894)

Vinegars & vegetables

BASIC SPICED VINEGAR FOR QUICK PICKLING

By varying the amount of sugar in this recipe, you can make *quick* sweet or sour pickles or pickled vegetables and fruits at any time. This vinegar will keep well for a long time, if properly stored.

The virtue of this Basic Spiced Vinegar is that it has been aged before using; thus, when poured over the food to be pickled, it will yield a product ready to be eaten soon. Quick-pickled products should be kept in the refrigerator.

2 quarts distilled white vinegar
salt to taste
sugar:
    1 cup for sour pickles
    2 cups for medium-sour pickles
    4 to 6 cups for sweet pickles and
      fruit pickles

Put in a spice bag of muslin:
    1-1/2 teaspoons allspice
    1-1/2 teaspoons cloves
    1/2 stick cinnamon
    1/2 piece mace, or 1/4 teaspoon
      ground mace
(other pickling spices to taste)

Boil the sugar, vinegar and spices for 15 minutes. Cool, cover and set aside for 2 weeks or more before removing spice bag. Use an earthenware or glass jar for holding the product. Spiced vinegar that is used soon after making needs more spice.

This most versatile vinegar (adapted from the Washington State Agricultural Extension Service) can be used in many ways. Use your imagination. For example:

Pick cucumbers of medium size, if you wish to pickle them whole, or large ones which you should slice or split. Wash well. Soak overnight in a brine of 1/2 cup pickling salt to 4 quarts water. Drain and rinse very well. If you use whole cucumbers pierce both ends and the middle with a knitting needle. This will allow the solution to penetrate thoroughly so that the pickling process will be hastened. Bring the necessary amount of vinegar (to cover) to a boil. Pour over pickles. Seal without heating the lids (so that you can sample them from time to time to see when they are ready—probably a week or two). Store in refrigerator.

SPICED VINEGAR

1 quart cider vinegar
1 to 2 tablespoons celery seed (1/2 ounce)
1/3 cup dried parsley
2 cloves garlic, pressed
3 small onions, chopped

3 whole cloves
1 teaspoon whole peppercorns
1 teaspoon grated nutmeg
1 tablespoon sugar
1 tablespoon brandy
pickling salt to taste

Put all ingredients into a sterilized jar and cover. Let stand for 3 weeks; then strain, pour into sterilized bottles and seal according to directions in ABC's.

CUCUMBER VINEGAR

10 large cucumbers or 12 smaller ones
1 quart vinegar
2 onions

2 shallots
1 tablespoon pickling salt
2 tablespoons pepper
1/4 teaspoon cayenne

Pare and slice the cucumbers, put them in a stone jar or wide-mouthed bottle with the vinegar; slice the onions and shallots, and add them, with all the other ingredients, to the cucumbers. Let them stand 4 or 5 days. Boil it all up and then let cool. When cold, strain the liquor through a piece of muslin, and store it away in small bottles well sealed. This vinegar is a very nice addition to gravies, hashes, etc., as well as a great improvement to salads, or poured over cold meat.

QUEEN VICTORIA'S CELERY VINEGAR

1 quart finely chopped celery, or 1/4
    pound celery seed (about 1-1/8 cups)

1 quart white vinegar
1 tablespoon pickling salt
1 tablespoon sugar

Put the celery or seed into a sterilized jar. Heat the vinegar, salt and sugar and pour boiling hot over the celery. Let cool, cover tightly and set away for 2 weeks. Strain, pour into sterilized bottles and seal according to the directions in ABC's.

GRANDMA GUTHRIE'S PICKLED BEETS

Select small young beets. Break off the stems (which can be cooked and eaten like spinach). Leave about an inch of the stem so that the beets do not bleed during cooking. Cook until just tender. Dip into cold water. Peel off skins. Discard stems. Large beets should be treated the same way, but slice to thickness desired. Make a syrup in the following proportions to cover:

2 cups sugar
2 cups cider vinegar
2 cups purified water
1/2 to 1 teaspoon salt, or to taste

1 teaspoon cloves
1 teaspoon whole allspice
1 tablespoon ground cinnamon
grated horseradish to taste

Pour over small beets and boil about 10 minutes. If you are using sliced large ones, test with fork so you don't overcook the slices. Pour hot into sterilized jars and seal at once according to instructions in ABC's.

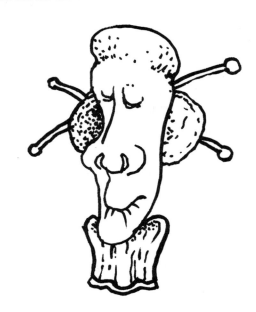

PICKLED EGGPLANT

small eggplants
table or pickling salt
cider vinegar
1/2 cup olive oil per quart jar

1/2 cup light vegetable oil per quart jar
pressed garlic
crushed oregano
crushed hot red pepper

This recipe calls for imagination and a fine Italian hand in distributing the condiments. Select rather small eggplants (about 1-pound size) or only one if you wish. Pare and slice thinly, no more than 1/4 inch thick. Salt each slice on both sides. Spread on paper or cloth towels and cover with a heavy weight overnight to remove excess juice.

Boil enough cider vinegar to cover the slices. Put them in the boiling vinegar for 1 minute only. Remove slices and squeeze out the excess vinegar between towels.

Make a mixture, about 1 cup per sterilized quart jar, of half olive oil and half light vegetable oil. Now comes the need for imagination and the fine hand. Pour a little oil into a quart jar. Put in a slice of eggplant, sprinkle with squeezed garlic, crushed oregano and crushed hot red pepper to your taste. Cover with a little more oil. Continue to alternate slices of eggplant with spices and oil until the jar is full.

Cover the jar and let it stand for at least a month before eating. The color will darken considerably. Do not refrigerate for this will harden the oil. This recipe seems to last indefinitely if you can keep your hands off the slices! Great hors d'oeuvre.

MATING MIXED PICKLED VEGETABLES

This title does not refer to the sex habits of vegetables. Although recent research has shown that vegetables have emotions (vegetarians beware), as yet we know little of their mating habits. Rather this title refers to a general recipe for putting them together. There are so many recipes for pickling carrots, cauliflower, celery, etc. separately that a basic one which can be used to pickle vegetables both separately and together is handy. Using the following general recipe, you may be moved by your imagination to plumb greater pickling depths.

2 to 3 large green bell peppers (or mixed with sweet red peppers)
small white onions, peeled
cloves of garlic
2 cups carrots, split or cut into pretty shapes

1 medium-size cauliflower, cut in flowerettes
4 to 5 stalks celery
2 large pickling cucumbers, sliced
green and black olives
strips of pimiento

Core peppers and blanch whole by dipping just in and out of boiling water and plunging immediately into ice water. When cool cut into strips. Peel onions and garlic; repeat blanching process. Blanch carrots, cauliflowerettes and celery the same way. Do not blanch cucumbers.

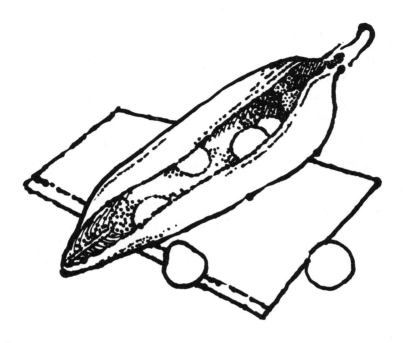

Pack cucumbers, carrots, celery, cauliflower and peppers carefully into about 4 sterilized quart jars. (You can always use what is left over for a salad that night.) Place in each quart jar any combinations of the onions, olives, pimiento and garlic that you desire.

5 cups (1-1/4 quarts) Basic Spiced Vinegar, page 115 (Choose whatever amount of sugar you wish.)

5 cups (1-1/4 quarts) purified water
1/2 cup pickling salt, or to taste

Combine vinegar, water and salt and bring to a boil. Pour boiling over vegetables in the jars. Seal according to directions in ABC's. If you wish, process the jars in a hot water bath for 5 minutes, also according to directions in ABC's.

DANNY'S PICKLED CAULIFLOWER

1 head cauliflower (or about 3 cups
   flowerettes)
brine of 2 tablespoons table salt to
   1 cup water

1 tablespoon mixed pickling spices
3 cups cider vinegar
1 tablespoon honey
1 cup mixed black and green olives

Boil cauliflower head 7 minutes. Tear into flowerettes, keeping some of the green. Drain and cool. Soak in brine to cover for 1 to 2 days. Drain and rinse.
Boil pickling spices, vinegar and honey just until the honey is thoroughly dissolved and the spices have permeated the solution. Add more vinegar and honey if needed to fill jars. Put the cauliflower into the mixture and cook about 2 minutes. Taste; should be crisp. Put hot in jar or crock. Add olives; refrigerate. Will be ready to eat in a day or so but improves with age.
Makes 1 quart or more

DILLED GREEN BEANS

4 pounds green beans, whole (about
   4 quarts)
for each pint jar:
   1/4 teaspoon hot red pepper, crushed
   1/2 teaspoon mustard seed

1 dill head
1 clove garlic
solution of 5 cups cider vinegar to
   5 cups purified water and 1/2 cup
   pickling salt

Because the fuzzy surface of beans tenaciously holds dust and soil, make certain that you wash beans thoroughly. Drain. Cut into lengths to fill pint jars. Pack beans into sterilized jars. Add crushed pepper, mustard seed, dill heads and garlic. (Blanch garlic in hot water for 1 minute before placing in jar.)
Combine vinegar, water and salt. Heat to boiling. Pour boiling liquid over beans, filling to 1/2 inch of the top of jar. Seal according to instructions in ABC's. Process for 5 minutes in a boiling water bath according to instructions in ABC's.
Makes about 7 pints

PICKLED CABBAGE

1 head white or red cabbage, sliced
12 small onions, chopped
1 to 2 chili peppers, chopped

Basic Spiced Vinegar, for sour pickles
   (page 115)
pickling salt and pepper

Put cabbage in bowl and sprinkle lightly with salt. Let stand 24 hours, turning cabbage occasionally. Drain. Add spiced vinegar to cover, salt if needed, and pepper to taste. Put in jars with onions and pieces of chili peppers. Let stand 24 hours. This makes a marvelous hors d'oeuvre. You may vary spices as you choose. A sprinkle of dill weed adds greatly to the flavor.

Watermelon

ROSY WATERMELON RIND PICKLE

rind from a medium-sized watermelon
1 quart purified water
2 cups white sugar
1-1/2 cups corn syrup
1-1/2 cups cider vinegar

1 teaspoon pickling salt
1/2 cup maraschino cherries
1 lemon, thinly sliced
2 tablespoons ground cinnamon stick
1 tablespoon whole cloves

Trim off the green and red from melon rind. Cut white portion of rind in 1/2- or 1-inch cubes. Cover with purified water. Simmer until rind appears tender, about 15 minutes. Drain thoroughly. Combine sugar, corn syrup, vinegar, salt and cherries. Tie lemon and spices in cheesecloth bag and add to syrup. Simmer 10 minutes. Add the quart of water and melon rind. Heat to boiling. Remove spice bag. Simmer rind until it appears clear, about 35 to 40 minutes. With a slotted spoon put rind in hot sterilized jars, filling one jar at a time. Pour hot syrup in each jar as you go and seal each immediately according to directions in ABC's.

pickles

WATERMELON RIND PICKLE

5 pounds watermelon rind
1 tablespoon lime (calcium oxide)
1 gallon purified water
7-1/2 pounds white sugar

2 lemons
10 small pieces ginger root, grated,
   or to taste
1 teaspoon vanilla

Pare off green and red parts of the rind. Cut rind in strips 1 inch wide by 4 inches long. Dissolve lime in water and soak rind in solution overnight. Next morning drain, rinse, and discard solution. Cook rind, covered, in fresh purified water until it is a little tender.

For each pound of rind add 1-1/2 pounds sugar to liquid; add lemon and ginger. Cook rind in this mixture until it is amber-colored and syrup is thick. Stir in vanilla after cooling liquid slightly. Heat again. With a slotted spoon put rind in hot sterilized jars, doing one jar at a time. Pour hot syrup over pickles as you go and seal each immediately according to the directions given in ABC's.

XYZ's
of
gardening
for
pickles

Of composts shall the Muse disdain to sing?
Nor soil her heavenly plumes? The sacred Muse
Nought sordid deems, but what is base; not fair,
Unless true Virtue stamp it with her seal.
Then, planter, wouldst thou double thine estate,
Never, ah! never, be asham'd to tread
Thy dung-heaps.
   —James Grainger (1721-67), "Call to the Muse"

And so, our first questions to the future and sometimes gardeners are: What of your soil? What of your composts, fertilizers and dung-heaps?

If you have a plot that will grow weeds, it will grow vegetables when properly treated. Or, what of that great plot of grass? Turn it over. You can have a garden no more than 20 by 50 feet which will produce all you will need for pickling. Furthermore, there is no rule which says you can not mix your vegetables with flowers in their beds, provided the vegetables are not shaded by their more showy cousins.

In deciding where to place your garden, choose a spot which will get good sunlight 5 to 6 hours a day and which is away from trees whose roots will sap the soil. Spade it to the depth of at least 8 inches and rake. This should be done in very early spring or late fall.

FERTILIZERS, SOILS, COMPOSTS AND DUNG-HEAPS

The analysis of soils can be very tricky. There are kits you can use to test them, if you feel experimental. By and large it is easier to contact your local U.S. Department of Agriculture for information. If need be, send them a sample of soil, tell them what you wish to grow, and ask advice on what fertilizers are best for your area. A good plant nursery would no doubt be of help, too.

As a rough test of your soil, when it is dry in fall or early spring, see how well it runs through your fingers. If it is clod-like, buy a bag or two of builder's sand and mix in. Once you fertilize, the soil should be adequate for your crops. A good fertilizer just before you plant and after you have moistened the soil is one made of a fish emulsion. Simply mix 2 tablespoons to 1 gallon of water. Pour near your plants, not on! Be sparing and repeat in a month.

If you have just begun to garden, by all means start a compost heap. In the long run this is one of the best fertilizers. It is a real pity that garbage disposals were ever invented, for down the drain is going fertilizing gold. Save those food scraps!

In a corner of your yard, spread out leaves, cuttings, vegetable scraps, almost anything organic except bones which will lure the local dog. Take your egg shells, crack them up or mix with water in your blender. Pour this on. Sprinkle over this a layer of earth. Cover with a plastic throw sheet, and fix it down with bricks or stones. Each time you put in a layer of anything sprinkle with soil. Aerate from time to time by turning over the material. In a short time you'll have an excellent compost which will be dark and sweet earth-smelling. Work this into your garden from time to time. If you don't wish to bother with this long method, dig good holes between your rows of vegetables, and bury your scraps, excluding fish which cats will soon get at.

Dung-heaps are hard to come by these days. In Grandmother's day, they were the joy of the family Sunday ride in the country. A burlap bag and shovel were always at the ready in the trunk of the old car. Grandma was on the outlook and at her shattering shout we would all swoop down upon a roadside dung-heap or march to a bemused farmer's barnyard. She particularly sang the joys of chicken and sheep manure and was usually so profuse in her praise of the farmer's barnyard that we got our germinal gold for nothing.

Too many cars have put an end to the dung-heaps and created their own. But if you can buy a good manure in your locality, by all means use it, although only in the fall. If put on too strongly in the spring, it will burn your plants. Turn it in about one pound per square foot. While it will encourage weeds, even they are worth it.

ABOUT WORMS AND STONES

If you don't have good, fat worms in your garden, it isn't much of a garden, for they break up the soil (which helps aerate it) and produce their own fertilizers. Buy some worms from a fisherman's store, but be sure you tell him that you want earthworms and what you want them for. The look on his face will be worth the worms' price. Now, if they don't live and multiply, there *is* something wrong with your soil— probably not enough organic materials. Add peat moss and compost.

Don't remove all the stones from your soil, just the ones that are too big or ones that get in the way of a struggling little plant. In fact, if you can find pebbles or buy some large gravel, place some between the rows of plants. They will keep down the weeds. Equally important, they will absorb heat during the day and help raise the temperature around the plants at night. This will promote plant growth.

PLANTING, CULTIVATION AND WATERING

Gardens should be planted north to south so that all plants get their share of sun. If your garden is sloping see what you can do about terracing with bricks. Follow the rules under each plant given here for the distances between rows and cultivation; if you dig too closely to some shallow-rooted plants, you'll ruin them. When they are young, cultivate very gently and weed by hand.

Irrigating either by small trenches or with one of those plastic lengths of hose which give off water very slowly is best, particularly for tomatoes and cucumbers when in blossom. Water falling on the blossoms will cause them to fall off. Spray watering will often crack the ripening tomatoes and produce shallow root systems. Watering is best done early in the morning or when the sun is going down. Your climate will dictate how often and how much to water, of course.

ABOUT BUGS, PESTILENCES
AND OTHER NUISANCES

Crescendo

And pity the poor planter, when the blast,
Fell plague of Heaven! Attacks his waving gold.
. . . Though well-manured;
A richness through thy fields from Nature boast;
Though seasons pour; this pestilence invades;
Too oft it seizes the glad infant throng,
Nor pities their green nonage: their broad blades,
Of which the graceful wood-nymphs erst composed
The greenest garlands to adorn their brows,
First pallid, sickly, dry and wither'd show;
Unseemly stains succeed: which nearer view'd
By microscopic arts, small eggs appear,
Dire fraught with reptile life; alas, too soon
They burst their filmy goal, and crawl abroad,
Bugs of uncommon shape.

—Ibid.

These days with our ecological concerns, many pesticides are no longer used. An amusing story told by a friend involves an old household hint which called for placing cucumbers on kitchen shelves to chase off bugs. It turned out they did, for she learned from an authority that they had been treated in the garden with a strong poison, Paris green, commonly used in the old days.

Our recommendation for pest control is, once again, consult your local Department of Agriculture office. Each area has different pests and invasions. But here are some old methods which are now modern once again:

- Pick the bugs off by hand and drop in a can of kerosene. Look *under* leaves.
- Plant some marigolds between your plants. Bugs seem to dislike their odor. Basil planted next to tomatoes repels tomato-loving bugs; onions, garlic and chives are good for this too. Mint will keep away ants.
- Around your strong-stemmed plants, such as cabbages, peppers or tomatoes, spread a circle of wood ashes. Another method is to cut a collar out of cardboard about three inches wide and place around the stems. With cucumbers when babies, you can make a tent of cheesecloth over their hills. Tack to a wooden frame. This will protect them from the striped cucumber beetle. When the plants become crowded remove the frame.
- Spray your plants with a mixture of water and strong, old-fashioned laundry soap. Don't use detergents.
- Spray with a mixture of water and light tea.
- Spray with garlic spray. To make, grind 1 chopped onion, 1 teaspoon cayenne pepper, 3 garlic cloves and a little water in a blender. Add 4 cups water, let stand 24 hours; strain through a stocking.
- Spray with a mixture of 1 ounce Epsom salts to 1 gallon water and a little laundry soap. Soap will make solution stick to leaves.

While our advice on gardening for pickles by no means exhausts the subject, it is sufficient to get the novice gardener started. We again emphasize that you use the resources of the U.S. Department of Agriculture. From their booklets you can discover when to plant in your area and learn about other vegetables you may wish to plant.

We suggest that the beginner buy his seedlings from a reputable nursery rather than try to start his garden from seed. Dill is easily grown from seed, but the other plants, if not started in hotbeds, might prove terribly disappointing. When you become more secure in your gardening, it is great fun to use your own hotbeds.

CUCUMBERS AND ZUCCHINI

Cucumbers and zucchini are not difficult to grow, but they are warm-weather crops, very delicate, and do not like extreme heat. Use plenty of water. Once again consult the U.S. Department of Agriculture about the time to plant. Cucumber vines will produce fruit in about 60 to 70 days; zucchini in less time. Pick regularly so that the plants will continue producing fruit. Always irrigate. Do not touch the blossoms with water. If you plant some flowers for the bees, it will help in germination. Plant cucumbers away from zucchini and other squashes so they won't cross-pollinate. Cucumbers and zucchini may be planted either in rows or in a series of hills.

Varieties of Cucumber Seedlings to Buy
For table use: White Spine, Davis Perfect
For pickling: Chicago Pickling, National
   Pickling
Varieties of Zucchini Seedlings to Buy
Cocozelle, Caserta, Zucco, Greyzini,
   Chefini Hybrid

Spacing of Plants 18 inches (if planted in rows) (If seeds are used, plant 1 inch apart; thin to 18 inches apart when established.)
Spacing of Rows 4 to 5 feet

To plant these vegetables in hills, rake the earth into a hill about 4 to 5 feet square and about a foot high. The seedlings go in a circle 6 to 12 inches in diameter in the center of the hill. Put in 2 to 3 seedlings or at least 12 seeds, for there is an old saying that goes:

Two for the cutworm, one for the crow,
One for the beetle and four to grow.

When the plants are well established, thin down to about 3. You might try the weaker ones elsewhere, such as next to the garage, to see if they'll make it. It is depressing to throw away even weak plants.

The advantage to the hill system is that it is easier to water and to weed. Allow a great deal of space between the hills so that the plants can spread out. Cultivate carefully by hand at first, for if the weeds take over you'll never win.

CABBAGE

Cabbage is not an easy vegetable to grow and is a cool-weather crop which will not tolerate heat or lack of water. Find out the time to plant it in your area from a nursery or the U.S. Department of Agriculture. Since it takes 95 to 140 days to reach maturity, it must be planted early. Make certain during a heat spell that it has plenty of water.

Cultivate both between the rows and around this plant. At first do so deeply, but as they begin to grow cultivate shallowly so as not to break a plant's root system.

Varieties of Seedlings to Buy
Copenhagen Market
Golden Acre
Glory of Enkhuizean (great for
    sauerkraut)
Spacing of Plants
Early: 12 to 15 inches apart
Late: 18 to 24 inches apart
Spacing of Rows
Early: 24 to 30 inches
Late: at least 30 inches

ONIONS

Buy your onion sets from a nursery and plant when the weather is cool and moist. They mature best when the weather is hot and dry. Can be used in 6 to 8 weeks, or if you wish them ripe, in about 14 weeks. Water well.

Varieties of Sets to Buy
Yellow Globe Danvers
Yellow, White or Red Southport Globe
Riverside Sweet Spanish

Spacing and Depth for Sets
3 to 4 inches apart and 1 to 2 inches in depth
Spacing of Rows 12 to 14 inches

Cultivation should be done frequently. Onions do not like weeds about; hand weed.

PEPPERS

Peppers are a tender warm-weather crop. Again consult the U.S. Department of Agriculture about when to set out your seedlings. Cool weather helps them when the flower buds and blossoms are forming. They like much water. Will bear in about 3 months.

Varieties of Seedlings to Buy
Sweet type: Ruby King, California Wonder, King of the North (All are deep green when young, turning red when well-ripened.)

Hot type: Celestial (long red), Cayenne, Coral Gem (red chili), Hungarian Wax (hot yellow)
Spacing of Plants 18 inches
Spacing of Rows 2 feet

Deep cultivation should be avoided. Work dirt up to stem. Cultivate often.

TOMATOES

Tomatoes are a warm-season, long-maturing crop. Again consult the U.S. Department of Agriculture about the time for planting your seedlings, which you definitely should buy from a nursery. When young they do badly in cool-damp weather. They love temperatures between 65° and 85°. Irrigate to prevent damage to the flowers or fruit and do so often.

Varieties to Buy
Early: Bonny Best and Earliana
Mid-season: Marglobe, Rutgers, Pritchard

Late: Stone Certified, Greater Baltimore Certified, Ponderosa, Golden Queen (yellow)

Spacing and Staking: 18 inches apart with rows 3 to 4 feet depending upon whether or not they are staked. In staking, place a pole next to the plant when planting. Tie it up as it grows with twine that will not damage the stems; pluck off sucker stems (between main branches) sparingly and with care.
Cultivate carefully because tomatoes have a shallow root system.

DILL

Dill can be planted from seed and grows well in sun anywhere. When seed heads are almost mature but not quite falling, cut and tie in bunches. Hang upside-down in a dry place until ready for use. If you wish, you may use the fresh dill heads.

GARLIC

Considering the cost of garlic today, it would pay you to plant a few cloves which are beginning to put out a bit of green. You will get many times the number of cloves you plant, and they will be strong. Plant when you do the onions. Mature in about 3 to 4 months. (Although sometimes, depending upon the climate, the maturing takes much longer.) Hang garlic by the stems until dry.

Index

Biographical Notes

RUBY CHARITY STARK GUTHRIE The recipes in this book, with a few exceptions, are a Stark family heritage, handed down from generation to generation, as this family of peripatetic pioneers moved westward. And the history of the Stark family is as old as America itself. Ruby Stark Guthrie's great-great grandfather, General John Stark, was the hero of the Battle of Bennington, where the British were decisively turned back from New England. Before that battle he said, "Tonight the American flag floats from yonder hill or Molly Stark sleeps a widow." Whether or not Molly Stark had packed a pickle in the General's knapsack to sustain his valor was not recorded. The American flag that did float from yonder hill that night, though, was the handiwork of a young lady from another side of the family tree, Betsy Ross, first cousin of Ruby Stark's Grandmother Lewis.

The family's westward migration ended in Oregon, where Ruby Charity Stark was born in 1898. In addition to being an accomplished cook, pickler, canner and gardener—as were all pioneer women—she possesses a myriad of other talents, one of them quite unusual for a woman of her day. In the 1930's she helped organize the first "all-girl" band in Ohio, in which she played the drums and was an expert at whistling in harmony. Even now, in her 70's, she is an avid painter, working mostly in watercolors, and a prolific restorer and decorator of furniture and "junk." She presently lives in Spokane where she maintains a large garden and cans everything she can lay her hands on.

JACK STARK GUTHRIE is Ruby Charity Stark Guthrie's son. His forte is writing and his chief contribution to this book was compiling and editing the family recipes. But he also shares his mother's passion for canning, pickling, bread-making and "junking." Born and raised in the State of Washington, he graduated from Reed College in history and received a master's degree in literature from the University of Washington, in addition to studying at the Sorbonne in Paris and the C. G. Jung Institute in Zurich. He has taught in private high schools, the University of Washington, University of Montana and San Francisco State College where he conducted a course in psychology and literature. He is the author of *A Diary for Dreams,* based on the psychology of Jung, and is currently working on a new book, *A Child's Guide to Adult Psychology and Other Mysteries.* He presently lives in San Francisco, where—between batches of pickles and sauerkraut—he operates a small publishing company specializing in works related to Jungian psychology.

RICHARD CALVO A native New Yorker, Richard Calvo relished comix in his early youth and collected, among others, *Mad, Classics Illustrated* and the E.C. gore-and-horror publications. A *Classics Illustrated* version of Joyce's *Ulysses* impressed him profoundly and influenced him to read the full-length original when he was 14; by 18, he had put aside his coded comix and dedicated himself to an unexpurgated life of "silence, exile and cunning." Since then he has held a wide variety of clerical positions and also found time during rounds of unemployment to study graphic design at Brooklyn's Pratt Institute, from which he received a degree in fine art. He now resides in San Francisco, where he is currently at play on the writing and picturing of a children's storybook for grown-ups.